ONCE UPON A RHYME

IMAGINATION FOR
A NEW GENERATION

Yorkshire & Lincolnshire
Vol II

Edited by Donna Samworth

 Young**Writers**

First published in Great Britain in 2004 by:
Young Writers
Remus House
Coltsfoot Drive
Peterborough
PE2 9JX
Telephone: 01733 890066
Website: www.youngwriters.co.uk

SB ISBN 1 84460 630 9

Foreword

Young Writers was established in 1991 and has been passionately devoted to the promotion of reading and writing in children and young adults ever since. The quest continues today. Young Writers remains as committed to engendering the fostering of burgeoning poetic and literary talent as ever.

This year's Young Writers competition has proven as vibrant and dynamic as ever and we are delighted to present a showcase of the best poetry from across the UK. Each poem has been carefully selected from a wealth of *Once Upon A Rhyme* entries before ultimately being published in this, our twelfth primary school poetry series.

Once again, we have been supremely impressed by the overall high quality of the entries we have received. The imagination, energy and creativity which has gone into each young writer's entry made choosing the best poems a challenging and often difficult but ultimately hugely rewarding task - the general high standard of the work submitted amply vindicating this opportunity to bring their poetry to a larger appreciative audience.

We sincerely hope you are pleased with our final selection and that you will enjoy *Once Upon A Rhyme Yorkshire & Lincolnshire Vol II* for many years to come.

Contents

Tom Bearpark (8)   1

Althorpe & Keadby Primary School, Scunthorpe
Jason Jones (11)   2
Holly Willerton (11)   2
Eddie Fowles (11)   3
Jack O'Callaghan (11)   3
Daisy Vollans (11)   4
Liam Coultard (10)   4
Larissa Giles (11)   5
Adam Ramsey (10)   5
Lucy Renton (11)   6

Angram Bank Primary School, Sheffield
Ashley Jacobs (11)   7
Ashley Jacobs (11) & Luke Pitcher (10)   8
Luke Pitcher (10)   9

Canon Peter Hall CE Primary School, Immingham
Ivymay Smith (8)   10
Terri-Lee Brewster (8)   10
Ashley Easton (11)   10
Katie Watters (8)   11
Natasha Wright (9)   11
Lacey Sparkes (8)   11
Kiya Fraser (9)   12
Adrienne Cooney (9)   12
Darwin Grey (8)   13
Lewis Richardson (8)   13
Shannon McBride (8)   14
Steven Styles (8)   14
Laura Tetley (10)   15
Curtis Pisarkiewicz (9)   15
Keileigh Louise Avis (11)   16
Stefan Allan (10)   16
Jacob Lumsden (11)   17
Simone Whale (10)   17

Chelsey Wherell (10)   18
Leigh Harrison (10)   18

Eckington Junior School, Sheffield

Beth Lake (10)   19
Emma Cranfield (11)   19
Sam Jarvis (11)   20
Jonathan Terry James Briggs (11)   20
Mathew Taylor (11)   20
Anna Marie Hibbert (11)   20
Sarah Beckett (11)   21
Daniel Batterham (11)   21
Craig Paul Collins (11)   21
Nicholas David Gelsthorpe (10)   21
Kiri Ann Rivett (10)   22
Melissa Vingoe-Wright (10)   22
Charlotte Parkin (11)   23
Alice Winckle (10)   23
Adam Broad (11)   24
Thomas Parker (11)   24
Carla Askwith (11)   25
Isabel Laycock (10)   25
Nicole Newton (11)   26
Katie Yates (11)   26
Alex Lacey-Hatton (11)   27
Ashleigh Jordan (11)   27
Samantha Jayne Walsh (11)   28
Rebecca Webster (11)   29
Abbie Jones (8)   29
Hannah Louise West (9)   30
Megan Sanders (10)   30
Katie May (11)   30
Matthew Alcock (11)   31
Jack Walker (11)   31
Adam James Cox (9)   31
Rebecca Saunby (9)   32
Ismay Gavelle (9)   32
Sheridan Eusman (10)   32
Ashley Roberts (9)   33
Kurt Price (9)   33
Tom O'Hara (8)   33

Field Lane J&I School, Batley

Hasib Afzal	34
Aamira Pandor & Rebekah (11)	35
Ammaarah Chhibda	35

Humberston CE Primary School, Grimsby

Joanne Bailey (11)	36
Kieran Tynan (8)	37
Lucy Telford (10)	37
Lorna Stafford (11)	38
Matthew Bailey (9)	38
Saskia Wilbourne-Davy (7)	39
Joshua Winchester (7)	39
Bethany Mae Stanham (8)	40
Samuel Cavendish (8)	40
Max Allen (8)	41
Rosie Murphy (11)	41
Joseph Robinson (8)	42
Emma De Halle (8)	42
Georgia Strong (8)	42
Sydney Hutchison (7)	43
Paige Stafford (8)	43
Lucy Stables (8)	43
Jacob Gabbitas (9)	44
Alice Epton (9)	44
Steffan Puckey (9)	45
Daniel Fisher (11)	45
Emily Stanham (10)	46
Charlotte Robinson (10)	46
Michael Hutchison (10)	46
Billy King (9)	47
Lindsey Todd (10)	47
Jerome Harper (9)	47
Faye Costello (8)	48
Alice Downes (9)	48
Sarah Quinn (10)	48
Virginia Read (7)	49
Joseph Steel (8)	49
Louis Townell (8)	49
Sophie Goldsmith (7)	49
Lauren Costello (10)	50

Emma Winn (10)   50
George Baker (10)   50
Bethaney Nicolson (9)   51
Holly Mavin (10)   51
Hannah Taylor (9)   51
Danielle Gilchrist (11)   52
Ellis Daniel Mortimore (11)   52
James Holliday (11)   52
Monketh Jaibaji (10)   53
Daniel Lond (11)   53
Stephen Ashton (11)   53
Karl Evardson (11)   54
Daniel Parker (11)   54
Paige Fenwick (9)   54
Nicola Bell (11)   55
Emily Pullan (11)   55
Melissa Balderson (10)   55
Abigail King (8)   56
Josephine Aitchison (10)   56
Daisy Gough (10)   56
David Low (11)   57
Alex Thompson (10)   57
Abbie Felton (11)   58
Jonathan Parker (11)   58

Leys Farm Junior School, Scunthorpe

Hannah Smith (9)   59
Imogen Culbert (9)   59
Charlotte Arrand (9)   60
Damien Henderson (9)   60
Eleanor Dawson (8)   61
Stephen Hutchinson (8)   61
Alex Todd (9)   62
Robert Peden (9)   62
Amelia Whiteside (9)   63
Lewis Dawson (9)   63
Lauren Darn (9)   64
Jodie Flynn (10)   65
Callum Thompson (9)   65
Amy Smith (9)   66
Kirsty Grey (9)   66

Charlie Cross 66
Freya Bradshaw (9) 67
Laura-Beth Ward (9) 67

Priory Lane Junior School, Scunthorpe
Kellie Martin (10) 68
Elizabeth Orwin (9) 68
Jessica Johnston (10) 69
Emily Mee (8) 69
Cameron Lee (9) 70
Jessica Wheeler (8) 70
Olivia Paige Graves (7) 71
Harry Pask (9) 71
Katy Harrison (9) 72
Abigail Corsair (8) 72
Rachel Wilson (10) 73
Nikki Koudis (9) 73
Meadow O'Connor (10) 74
Danielle Wilson (10) 75
Jessica Corsair (10) 76
Jessica Shaw (10) 77
Joe Toplass (10) 78
Hannah Spouge (9) 79
Jack Bower (10) 80
Meadow O'Connor (10) & Jessica Shaw (9) 81
Hannah Lavin (10) 82
Hannah Turner (9) 83
Scott Strong (9) 84
Paul Smith (9) 85
Matthew Kenyon (9) 86
William Green (10) 87
Ryan Prosser (10) 88

Rosehill Junior School, Rotherham
Helesha Thompson (10) 88
Racheal Dobson (10) 89
Jodie Ackerman (10) 89
Chelsea Waldby (9) 90
Ryan Gary Oxley (10) 90
Christopher Niel Smith (9) 91
Kyle Pitt (10) 91

Stacey Brown (10)	92
Terry Mitchell (10)	92
Lauren Draycott (10)	93
Chloe Darby (10)	94
Demi Wilkinson (8)	94
Olivia Davies (8)	95
Danielle Easson (8)	95
Aimee Jenkinson	96
Shelby Leigh Postans (9)	96
Emily Huddleston (9)	97
Luke Riley (10)	97
Bethany Casterton (9)	98
Sam Spink (10)	99
Alisia Angel (8)	100
Alexandra Hetherington (10)	100
Jack Sheeran (11)	101
Hannah Reeder (10)	101
Matthew Johnson (10)	102
Isabella Cullen (10)	102
Hayley Dudill (10)	103
Lauren Longson (9)	103
Amy Barrie (9)	104
Joshua Willows (9)	104
Aimee Morton (10)	105
Jana Thompson (10)	105
Lucie Tyler (10)	106
Sam Billups (10)	106
Sophie Whittam (11)	107
Lauren Bateman (8)	107
Joe Moore (7)	108
Elizabeth M Stringer (8)	108
Charly Manion (10)	108
Harry Attwood (8)	109
Rosie Price (9)	109
Bethany Watt (10)	109
Tyler David Scothern (8)	110
Chloe Mae Davies (8)	110
Luke Grainger (10)	111
Shellie O'Connor (8)	111
Alexandra Gregory (10)	112
Ashley Spooner (9)	113

Lauren Hudson (10)   113
Chloe Pashley (10)   114
Emma Harrington (8)   114
Jack Foss (8)   114
Joshua Gillespie (8)   115
Nicole Tonks (8)   115
Jack Oliver Dowell (10)   115
Olivia May Greenwood (8)   116
Micah Drakes (8)   116
Lauren Dickinson (10)   117
Joshua Mason (8)   117
Matthew Tonks (11)   118
Faye Braisby (8)   118
Jordan Battersby (9)   119
Brianna Staton (8)   119
Katie Spencer (10)   120
Jake Beavers (11)   121
Lewis Routledge (11)   122
Matthew Ambler (10)   122
Matt Allen (11)   123
Jordan Lowe (10)   123
Kieron Phillips (9)   124
Jessica Underwood (11)   125
Charlotte Stringer (11)   126
Adam Ian Bates (11)   127
Sophie Hughes (11)   128

St Joseph's RC Primary School, Halifax

Amy Illingworth (8)   128
Niall Cuttle (8)   129
Georgia Egan (11)   129
Ben Cole (11)   130
Clare Armstrong (9)   131
Robert Dickinson (9)   131
Laura Burton (9)   132
Charlotte Coyne (9)   132
Laura Whittaker (8)   133
John Paul Morrow (9)   133
Reece Fisher Lowry (9)   133
Hayley Keane (9)   134

Matthew Bartey (9)   134
Harriet Slater (9)   134
Joe McGinley (9)   135

Womersley CE Primary School, Doncaster
Sophie Coolledge (11)   135
Joshua Kneafsey (10)   136

The Poems

School Dinners

School dinners
are the winners,
you just can't beat
the school meat.

When it's coleslaw and curry
I'm in a hurry,
coleslaw and rice
is very, very nice.

Potatoes and mash
definitely aren't trash,
I always say, 'Yes please!'
when it's sweetcorn and peas.

When it's apple pie
I touch the sky,
cucumber and ice cream
make me stray into a dream.

Cake and steak
used to be fake,
but now it's home-made,
it's not trash like lemonade.

Tom Bearpark (8)

The Cornish Baker's Shop

I spent a moment in a baker's shop,
There were two big coolers, chilling pop,
With people laughing, talking and having a good time,
I heard the oven timer start to chime,
The freezer that was humming, with ice cream inside
And the last chocolate cake, was trying to hide,
Behind all the signs, saying 25% off,
It had chocolate chips and sprinkles on top,
The Cornish pasties' aroma was wafting around the room,
It was like a little ray of sunshine, coming through the gloom,
The steam was rising from the sausage rolls
And outside, the sun was beaming through the holes,
In the clouds that just seem to hang in the sky
And an advertising plane that was flying so high,
The slogans in the shop were ever so clever
And the first bite of a fresh bun, that will last forever.

Jason Jones (11)
Althorpe & Keadby Primary School, Scunthorpe

A Moment To Remember

This time was precious:
The smoothness of grass, showed the dew,
Laying down in the mystical garden of dreams,
The red ball of fire, brightly gleams,
The sun slowing rising from the east, the day is dawning,
The wind blowing gently, two in the morning,
The taste of a salad on the tip of your tongue,
Robin's merry song was sung,
The slowly rotting timber,
Butterflies awaken from their slumber,
The squeaking of a guinea pig,
The rustling of a rabbit rearranging twigs,
The taste of a summer salad,
This time was precious.

Holly Willerton (11)
Althorpe & Keadby Primary School, Scunthorpe

Trees In Summer

The tree is a floppy hand,
Waving its green leaves through the summer's breeze,

It's a hollow base,
Holding a giant army of bees inside,

It's a thick, metal bar,
For its trunk is difficult to chop down,

It's a gigantic fog of mist,
Casting a big shadow on the floor,

It's at the bottom of the food chain,
For people keep chopping them down,

It's the source of all lives,
For it gives off oxygen to things around it,

It's a person . . .
For it wrinkles as it gets older.

Eddie Fowles (11)
Althorpe & Keadby Primary School, Scunthorpe

The Things I Love . . .

The smell of delicious vanilla ice cream,
The smile on my mum's face when she's happy,
The orange on me from the sunset,
The smell of the salt in the sea,
The feel of the rough, sharp rocks,
The feel of the soft sand and the shiny shells,
The noise of my brother laughing at my dad,
The taste of hot dogs and ice cream,
The shouting of Mum when she's getting thrown in the sea,
The smell of the dead crab and
The noise of my dad laughing when we play cards.

Jack O'Callaghan (11)
Althorpe & Keadby Primary School, Scunthorpe

A Moment In Time

Rolling hills tumbling all around
The wind seems to whisper
A silent song to all who care to listen
The great lake Stickle Tarn
Lets ripples out, then catches them
Like a mother bringing in her children
The sun hangs as if on invisible wire
From the deep blue whitewashed sky
The smell of hot chocolate
Blows through the air filling the lungs
Of all who are around
Family and friends are stood in a buzz of chatter
But I just think and stare
Warmth and happiness is all around
From the tip of the sky
Right down to the ground
A moment in time ready to savour
In my mind it will never waver
It's my moment . . .

Daisy Vollans (11)
Althorpe & Keadby Primary School, Scunthorpe

Tree

It is a man, standing tall and proud.
Green, the inside of a kiwi.
Overhanging branches are dresses dragging across the floor.
It is as tall as a rocket.
Swaying, as if a train speeding past.
Leaves rustling as a paper bag.
Hands holding onto anything that falls.
Bark rough, like an old, wrinkled person.

Liam Coultard (10)
Althorpe & Keadby Primary School, Scunthorpe

The Tree

The tree is a person moving all the time
There are whistling birds swaying in the wind

The leaves are lots of hearts being held in the air
The sound of rustling papers

The branches are arms staying in one place
They are tinsel on a Christmas tree
They are skirts being trailed down to the ground

The trunks are elephant trunks
They are a scaly dragon's arm

The seeds are little babies being looked after
They are little bouncy balls being thrown into the air

The tree has got a mouth, letting out oxygen for us to breathe in
It has a heart letting out everything it's got.

Larissa Giles (11)
Althorpe & Keadby Primary School, Scunthorpe

Trees

A tree is a mysterious monster swaying from side to side in the wind,
The bark of a tree is its armour, tough and rough,
The dead leaves are the trees' litter for tiny animals' homes,
Trees living leaves are claws, snaring and snatching prey,
In winter you can see trees' scary pointed hands,
Their leaves are crisp packets crackling in the wind,
The trees' roots are bendy pipes sucking the land dry,
The future tree is a conker, protected by a sharp, spiky shell,
An acorn is a tiny tea cup, also a fresh meal for a squirrel,
Trees are here to live on.

Adam Ramsey (10)
Althorpe & Keadby Primary School, Scunthorpe

My Favourite Moment

At home with my family,
on Christmas Day,
Mum, Dad, dog and Grandma,
all waiting to play.

I can see all my presents
under the tree,
I hope there's something,
just for me.

I can smell Polos
and dog treats,
so can my family
all in their seats.

Out goes the wrapping paper
into the bag,
nothing is left,
not even a rag.

One parcel left
in the corner,
I wonder what it is
I feel like a sauna.

There, I unwrap it,
stood, was a machine,
already to be sang on,
but needing a clean.

I am so happy,
the day has come,
I can get ready,
to have some serious fun!

Lucy Renton (11)
Althorpe & Keadby Primary School, Scunthorpe

Scrooge

Marley floated right through the door
He said, 'More you must give to the poor'
These three spirits will show you how
Change your ways, now, now, now.

The past ghost came and took him back
To show him how much he had slacked
When he was at boarding school
His father hated him, he was a fool.

The present ghost took him to Cratchet's house
Where Tiny Tim sat quiet as a mouse
No money, his father, Bob Cratchet had
To mend the back of his little lad.

The future ghost showed Tim was dead
Nasty thoughts span round his head
When he woke, he decided to change
His maid thought it was all rather strange.

Mr Scrooge danced round and round
For the new love of Christmas he had found
After turkey and Christmas spud
He went to Cratchet's just like he should.

He gave some money for Tim's operation
Tim fell off his crutches in adoration
After that, he gave some more
Lots and lots of money to the poor
Scrooge will live life lots more.

Ashley Jacobs (11)
Angram Bank Primary School, Sheffield

Perseus' Quest

Years ago his mother did say
'There is a Gorgon on a rock, far away
You'll turn to stone if you catch her eye
Her scaly skin all green and dry.'

Polydektes, King of the land
He forced Danae to take his hand
In marriage till death do them part
That did not fit well in Perseus' heart.

The Gryi were the Gorgon's sisters
Their faces decaying and full of blisters
They gave him some valued information
'The nymphs will give you a transformation.'

He found the nymphs and he was gifted
With the winged sandals he was lifted
With the cap of invisibility
He had extraordinary super-ability.

On the way, he saw Atlas the giant
He holds up the heavens though he is defiant
His greatest wish is in Medusa's eyes
Whenever across the world she flies.

Invisible he landed at Medusa's lair
Through the shield he saw her venomous hair
Chanting she tried to make him look
But he could read her like a book.

'I'll take off her head with the blade of my sword
After Polydektes I shall be lord'
Always looking through the shield
He swings his sword, her head he wields.

He flies back with the head in a bag
He shows Atlas the head of a hag
Polydektes did not believe a word
He thought the whole idea was absurd.

Polydektes' servants had all fled
As he showed the lord the Gorgon's head
Perseus can now claim the throne
As he left Polydektes all alone.

Her scaly skin all green and dry
You'll turn to stone if you catch her eye
There was a Gorgon on a rock, far away
By Danae's son she was slain.

Ashley Jacobs (11) & Luke Pitcher (10)
Angram Bank Primary School, Sheffield

Macbeth

Macbeth had won the battle for,
King Duncan who wanted no more,
He was given the title Thane,
Little did he know, he would go insane.

On the way home to his wife,
He met the hags who changed his life,
They told him what his life would bring,
That he would become Scotland's king.

His wife was selfish and also jealous,
She wanted power with great zealous,
She persuaded him to kill the lord,
With a sharp and bloody sword.

Soon he was to be crowned,
People gather from all around,
When the crown was on his head,
He saw King Duncan lying dead.

He had visions at the feast,
People screaming, 'He is the beast!'
The queen told everyone to leave,
The Kkng was suffering major grief.

He fought in the battle and he slaughtered,
With blood the battlefield was watered,
At last he was against Macduff,
Macbeth was skilled, but Macduff was tough.

Luke Pitcher (10)
Angram Bank Primary School, Sheffield

Princess

P urple dresses, all around, emeralds, diamonds
R oses in the garden all around the pond with dolphin statues
I n the bedroom lies a witch with blue hair
N ear the kitchen is a white cat with a pink ribbon round her neck
C hristmas decoration
E ven when she goes out she has her diamonds all around her
S he has a blue ribbon round her neck
S cent of her roses smell like sugar and sweetness.

Ivymay Smith (8)
Canon Peter Hall CE Primary School, Immingham

Princess

P urple princess shining
R oses in the garden of the palace
I n the castle on the stairs, lies the witch with falling-out hair
N ear the bedroom lies the dragon waiting for the wagon
C astles have a scent of roses and poses
E ven when they're dirty
S ilver diamond sparkling
S unny castles look like emeralds in the sun.

Terri-Lee Brewster (8)
Canon Peter Hall CE Primary School, Immingham

Medieval Time

M ad knights killing each other
E veryone cheering for the knights
D ead people lying on the floor
I diots interrupt the fight
E vil enemies stab opponents
V icious, violent opponent kills enemy
A t last, enemy has been killed
L ots of blood pouring out.

Ashley Easton (11)
Canon Peter Hall CE Primary School, Immingham

King Henry

K ing Henry was a bad king
I n the beautiful castle was his wife
N o one really liked King Henry
G liding through the countries

H enry was an evil man
E ven he married six wives
N one of his wives were good for him
R eally, he shouldn't have been a king
Y elling, murdering, divorcing and too cruel to rule!

Katie Watters (8)
Canon Peter Hall CE Primary School, Immingham

The Dragon Fight

K ing Tom sent an army into the forest
N ight-time came and the knights had to fight the dragon
I n a small, deep, dark, black hole
G reat big swords, arrows and poles forced into the dragon
H eat came flying out of his mouth, he tried to fly
　　　　　　he had eaten a person whole before *he* died
T he dragon was dead on the floor, we threw him in the water
　　　　　　just in time to save my daughter.

Natasha Wright (9)
Canon Peter Hall CE Primary School, Immingham

Castles

C atherine Parr
A final wife for Henry
S he was 31 when she married him
T LC she gave him
L ost his fight to live
E dward V was the king, but not for long
S oon to be followed by his sister Elizabeth I.

Lacey Sparkes (8)
Canon Peter Hall CE Primary School, Immingham

Princess Adore

Princess stuck up in a tower,
the witch that left her has got power.
Running sounds of hooves tapping,
even a bit of witches' cackling.
In-between the big black stairs,
the witch is coming, oh do beware!
Nothing but power, nothing but lies
from the witch until she dies.
Coming closer and closer again,
She is coming you may experience some pain.
Even louder the footsteps come,
she is unlocking the door, oh no, not again!
Soon she is coming in the door.
she is coming for
the Princess Adore.
Sat down, the princess is with rosy-red cheeks
and shaking with fear,
sitting down with a diamond tear.

Kiya Fraser (9)
Canon Peter Hall CE Primary School, Immingham

Medieval

Castles were for very special people
And if the king and queen departed,
They had knights to protect the faint-hearted,
Servants to do all the work,
The king and queen were in charge of the people who went berserk,
Love didn't matter to Henry VIII,
Everyone in the Catholic Church didn't want to be his mate,
Henry killed some of his wives and took so many other lives.

Adrienne Cooney (9)
Canon Peter Hall CE Primary School, Immingham

The Fight Between Good And Evil

K ing Darwin sent an army in the
N ight to fight a dragon
 I n a dungeon with
G reat swords and axes
H ard armour and the king
T ore the dragon's neck
S tabbing with the swords

O h, but it didn't work
F ight continued between the good and the dark side

T he dark side seemed to be winning
H ope seemed to be lost
E nd was soon to become

K ing Darwin sent for some more men
 I n the dragon's dungeon
N o one could kill the dragon, but
G reat, brave King Darwin took them back to the light.

Darwin Grey (8)
Canon Peter Hall CE Primary School, Immingham

King Henry

H enry had six wives
E meralds and jewels he gave them
N o wife was good enough for him; a son was what he wanted
R ich he was
Y ellow-gold was his favourite colour
S orry was he, when his son Edward died

W hen he wanted something he got it, a divorce or a beheading
'I will help you,' said one wife
V ery sad when he died
E lizabeth was the last Tudor
S o no king to rule the land.

Lewis Richardson (8)
Canon Peter Hall CE Primary School, Immingham

King Henry VIII

S is for six wives of Henry VIII
I is for old inns in medieval times
X is for no X-rays when Henry was around

W is for witches, which weren't even real
I is for itches which everyone always had
V is for victory of the knights
E is for Elizabeth I, his daughter
S is for the scurrying servants carrying water!

O h Henry was a bad king
F or he married six times

H e beheaded and divorced his wives
E ven the pope told him no
N ever did Henry listen
R ain came through the dungeon roof
Y ou had to have a shield and a sword and food to horde!

Shannon McBride (8)
Canon Peter Hall CE Primary School, Immingham

King

K ing Henry was a killer
I n the 16th century
N oblemen and knights rode on their horses
G uards were guarding the king's gates

H enry VIII married six wives
E nemy of Rome he became
N ot happy until he had a son
R uled the Church of England
Y ears of waiting for a son, didn't make him happy.

Steven Styles (8)
Canon Peter Hall CE Primary School, Immingham

Walking, Stumbling, Climbing

Walking through the tower,
Hour by hour,
Stumbling over chains,
Covered with pains,
Climbing to the top of castles,
Hearing noises and rustles,
Putting on my suit of armour,
Ready for the big day.

Walking back down the tower,
Taking it slowly hour by hour,
Stepping over hanging chains,
Getting rid of all my pains,
Climbing down from tops of castles,
Hearing those noises and rustles,
Clanging my suit of armour,
Here is the big day.

Laura Tetley (10)
Canon Peter Hall CE Primary School, Immingham

Snow White

S now White is a pretty girl
N ow the seven dwarves live with her
O h no, the witch has come
W hen the dwarves get home they think she is dead

W hen the prince came, she came alive
H er friends were happy
I n her bed there were some flowers
T hen she kissed the dwarves goodbye
E veryone started to cry.

Curtis Pisarkiewicz (9)
Canon Peter Hall CE Primary School, Immingham

I'm The Knight In Shining Armour

I'm the knight in shining armour, I'm going to save the day,
Don't worry boys and girls, I'm on my way,
Running up the staircase, my armour going clang,
Opening and closing the doors, bang, bang, bang,
My heart is beating fast, the scream is getting louder,
My face is as white as powder.
I'm the knight in shining armour, I'm coming to save the day,
Don't worry boys and girls, I'm on my way,
A fire-breathing dragon is outside the door,
I'm feeling I want to run away, more, more, more,
I open the door, fire roars out,
I feel like I want to shout, shout, shout.
I'm the knight in shining armour, I'm supposed to save the day,
I'm sorry boys and girls, but I'm going to run, run, run away.

Keileigh Louise Avis (11)
Canon Peter Hall CE Primary School, Immingham

Medieval Castle

Medieval castles stand tall,
The guards at the top take care not to fall,
The king sits on a throne,
While the farmers moan.

Castles defend the ground,
Outside you can't hear a sound,
Castles show great power,
They can even withstand a rain shower.

The moat gleams in the sun,
If in a castle you don't fear a gun,
But the time of castles came to an end,
However, they may be back, just round the bend.

Stefan Allan (10)
Canon Peter Hall CE Primary School, Immingham

My Medieval Poem

A knight is on his horse,
He's riding into battle,
Using all his force.

Farmer and his cattle,
Running to his barn,
All he wants is to flee from his farm.

Charging down each other,
Knocking them to the ground,
They're doing it to defend the one who's been crowned.

The farmer is safe,
He's shivering with terror,
He could not think of a more safer place.

The battle is over,
Justice has been done,
Now they're all off home for a hot-cross bun.

Jacob Lumsden (11)
Canon Peter Hall CE Primary School, Immingham

Cinderella

A pretty girl lives,
With her evil stepsisters,
All day she must clean,
The sisters are mean,
She will not go to the ball,
In the great big hall,
Her fairy godmother comes to her rescue,
'Hello,' they say politely,
'We like you slightly,
How are you dear?'
My evil stepsisters are the ones I fear.

Simone Whale (10)
Canon Peter Hall CE Primary School, Immingham

The Three Little Bears

We are the three little bears,
We live in a cottage.
There is a little girl who came in our house
And she crept like a mouse.
She has golden hair
And a big, blue puffy dress.
Small, red little shoes
And a little red bow.
She ate all of our porridge,
That we'd left in our cottage.
She broke our chairs
And then she went upstairs.
In our bed,
With my ted.
We came in
And then she came out
And then we shouted,
'Get out!'

Chelsey Wherell (10)
Canon Peter Hall CE Primary School, Immingham

Arthur, King Of Britain

I know a man from history,
His name is Arthur King,
He lives in a castle upon the hills,
So he was always seen.

His metal, shiny armour,
Protects him from the dragon's flames,
He once was fried, but is still alive,
Now that's a king of Britain!

Leigh Harrison (10)
Canon Peter Hall CE Primary School, Immingham

A Bag Full Of Hippos

A bag full of hippos
A cup full of dogs
A mouth full of flippers
A book full of frogs.

A vase full of lightning
A window full of tadpoles
A ballet dancer which is fighting
A hand full of happy soles.

A gun full of snails
A box full of orange cats
A pocket full of whales
A thimble full of bats

A pencil full of clocks
A bin full of rain
A ruler full of foxes
Walking down the lane!

Beth Lake (10)
Eckington Junior School, Sheffield

War

Rolling countryside, trees green, lush
Armies march to the campsite
Rumbling planes, fear
Cornfields turned into trenches, mud, not grass, tanks, not animals
Barbed wire, not hawthorn hedges
More tanks move in, guns in the distance, in place of birds' songs
Bombs sound like drums in the deep blackness
Smoke and flames
The world's worst nightmare
Death and famine spread like a hand on the earth
The armies charge on the final push, both sides, all die
If this is making peace, then what is war?

Emma Cranfield (11)
Eckington Junior School, Sheffield

Winter Haiku

Black ice on the roads,
White snowmen hug with stick arms
Snow falls like white leaves!

Sam Jarvis (11)
Eckington Junior School, Sheffield

Winter Haiku

Building cold snowmen
Throwing snowballs at your friends
Slide on icy roads.

Jonathan Terry James Briggs (11)
Eckington Junior School, Sheffield

Summer Haiku

The morning brightens
The sun awakes from the night
And the day gets hot.

Mathew Taylor (11)
Eckington Junior School, Sheffield

Summer Haiku

You can play a game
You can get an ice cream cone
You can get a tan.

Anna Marie Hibbert (11)
Eckington Junior School, Sheffield

The Enchanted Stallion Haiku

Hooves thud in meadows
Strong head and expressive eyes
It's no illusion.

Sarah Beckett (11)
Eckington Junior School, Sheffield

Winter Haiku

Silent snowmen smile
Swirvy snowboards slip and slide
Blustery blizzards.

Daniel Batterham (11)
Eckington Junior School, Sheffield

Summer Haiku

The sun gets angry
Sea waves at the lonely sky
The sun can burn you.

Craig Paul Collins (11)
Eckington Junior School, Sheffield

Winter Haiku

Lovely roast chicken
Dogs after snowmen's stick arms
Snow drifts like paper.

Nicholas David Gelsthorpe (10)
Eckington Junior School, Sheffield

My Family

In our family
Dad is a bacon butty
He is a pair of combat trousers
He is the rope on a wrestling ring
And he is the laughing hyena in the woods.

In our family
Mum is the noisy vacuum cleaner
She is the gardener in spring
She is the pillow for my head
And she is the don't which I wish was a do.

In our family
Bret is the wacky clown
He is the soft bowl of sweetcorn
He is the bowl of Weetos on the floor
He is the winner at Monopoly.

And that leaves me
Gorgeous, bossy, intelligent
The best of all the lot!

Kiri Ann Rivett (10)
Eckington Junior School, Sheffield

The Tiger

The tiger
The predator
Fierce, soft, furious
Like a fluorescent light in the night
Like a shark catching its prey
It makes me feel cautious
Like a grasshopper in the grass waiting to be stood on
The tiger
Reminds us what is out there.

Melissa Vingoe-Wright (10)
Eckington Junior School, Sheffield

Going Home

On my way home I saw
A lion with two heads
A glove with three fingers
A giraffe with no neck.

On my way home I saw
A book without pages
A car with no wheels
A drawing moving.

On my way home I saw
Some glasses with no lenses
A pen with no nib
A house with no light.

On my way home
I don't think
I'll be going that way again.

Charlotte Parkin (11)
Eckington Junior School, Sheffield

Mrs Metaphor

Mrs Metaphor is a warm cup of tea
A red fluffy slipper
A night by the fire.

Mrs Metaphor is a milky bowl of cornflakes
A pink towelling dressing gown
A fresh glass of orange juice.

Mrs Metaphor is a green watering can
A yellow daffodil
A tall washing line.

Mrs Metaphor is a cosy bedroom
A warm quilt
A good night's sleep.

Alice Winckle (10)
Eckington Junior School, Sheffield

The Viper GTS, The Ford Fiesta

The fast Viper GTS
Made in America
Big, fast, furious
Like Concorde zooming down the runway
Like a speck on the horizon getting closer by the second.
It makes me feel powerless
Like a king with no power
The fast Viper GTS
Reminds me of how rubbish Ford Fiesta's are
The Ford Fiesta
Made in Germany
Slow, small, sharp
Like a turtle walking slowly
Like time has stopped
I feel ashamed
Like a man with no car
The Ford Fiesta
Reminds me of how cool a Viper GTS is.

Adam Broad (11)
Eckington Junior School, Sheffield

The Great Wall Of China

The Great Wall of China
Built millions of years ago
Long, strong, tall
Like a long road reaching across the world
Like a long wall that makes the world in two halves
It makes me feel lonely
Like I'm being ignored
The Great Wall of China
Reminds us how long our life is.

Thomas Parker (11)
Eckington Junior School, Sheffield

Dog Kennings

Tail flicker
Soppy kisser
Gentle player
Curled-up layer
Bum smeller
Secret teller
Fast runner
Eating stunner
Paw giver
Long liver
Water lapper
Ear flapper
Excited walker
Noisy talker.

Carla Askwith (11)
Eckington Junior School, Sheffield

Sound

Dogs bark
People talk

Babies cry
Adults pry

Rain drips
Paper rips

Mowers buzz
Children fuss

You can't see sound
But you know it's around.

Isabel Laycock (10)
Eckington Junior School, Sheffield

An Upside Down World

A pack of trees
A dump of flowers
A swarm of kittens
A shoal of towers.

A school of pipes
A gaggle of bins
A scrum of pens
A peal of tins.

A reel of paper
A box of teachers
A ream of rubbers
A cluster of breeches.

Nicole Newton (11)
Eckington Junior School, Sheffield

Possible Things

A mouse full of giants
A basket full of time
A head full of English books
As the cat sits down to dine.

A rat at a football match
A lion at a school
A forgetful owl
An elephant so cool.

A word calculator
A vegetarian bat
A football team of elephants
And clumsy scored that.

Katie Yates (11)
Eckington Junior School, Sheffield

My Family

My dad is the spanner out of a tool box,
he is the Chinese out of a take-away,
he is the twist of a twister,
he is the wool of the carpet.

My mum is the imagination out of a brain,
she is the tidiness of a house,
she is the rocks of a mountain,
she is the clothes of a washing machine.

My brother is the sugar out of a sweet
he is the screen of a TV,
he is the disc of a PlayStation,
he is the pillow of a bed.

Alex Lacey-Hatton (11)
Eckington Junior School, Sheffield

A Shopping Spree

Shop, shop, until you drop
Shop, shop, no time for pop
Get to the sales
Local, not Wales
Shop, shop, until you drop.

Shop, shop, until you drop
Don't waste your time cleaning with a mop
New Look, Select, hear the tills ping
Don't go to the church to have a sing.

A shopping spree is mad
A shopping spree is wild
After that, you'll be sleeping like a child.

Ashleigh Jordan (11)
Eckington Junior School, Sheffield

What Is Colour?

(Based on 'What Is Pink?' by Christina Rossetti)

What is purple?
Some pencil cases are purple in
      the classroom light
and a sugary sweet that melts
      in the night.

What is green?
Green is the colour of my
      friend's eyes
and a grain of grass on the
      floor to look like flies.

What is blue?
Blue is the colour of the sky
      on a sunny day
and the pool on holiday
      or so I say.

What is red?
Red is a rose at a Valentine's
      meal
and a warm fire after you've
      made a deal.

What is yellow?
Yellow is a lemon just picked
      off a tree
and the gazing light saying,
      'Look at me.'

Samantha Jayne Walsh (11)
Eckington Junior School, Sheffield

A Haiku For All Seasons

Dew hangs like crystals
The big blanket covers ground
Icicles shiver.

Flowers open up
Lambs dance to silent music
Hill's hair sways slowly.

Sun smiles, teeth glow bright
Flowers' heads turn, green hands wave
Wind whistles gently.

Balding trees worry
Traffic light leaves change colour
Loud pumpkins cackle.

Rebecca Webster (11)
Eckington Junior School, Sheffield

Summer Is . . .

The sound of the Jacuzzi bubbles popping
all around me.
The taste of ice cream melting softly
on my tongue.
The touch of my fluffy dog
sitting on my lap.
The sight of seagulls flying
in the summer breeze.
The smell of melting chocolate
melting slowly.
Summer is . . . all of these.

Abbie Jones (8)
Eckington Junior School, Sheffield

Summer Is . . .

The taste of a soft ice lolly
on my hot throat.
The sound of newborn baby birds
tweeting in their nests.
The smell of burning sausages
on a busy barbecue.
The feel of the summer breeze
on my hot, burning neck.
The sight of grass swaying
from side to side on a summer's day.
Summer is . . . all of these.

Hannah Louise West (9)
Eckington Junior School, Sheffield

Summer

S is for the sun shining brightly
U is for the universe which is having fun
M is for marigolds in the sun
M is for merry-go-rounds which go round and round
E is for entertainment in the back garden
R is for refreshments that taste so good.

Megan Sanders (10)
Eckington Junior School, Sheffield

Summer Haikus

Blazing sun shines down
Seas glitter and boats are out
Children are boiling.

Suncream and sun hats
Children having water fights
Eating cold ice creams.

Katie May (11)
Eckington Junior School, Sheffield

The Poetry Machine: Snakes

The slithering snake
Mouth opens wide
Long, strong, fast
Like a stick on a tree
Like a cave opening wide
It makes me feel short
Like a short person surrounded by long snakes
The slithering snake
Reminds me how long things are.

Matthew Alcock (11)
Eckington Junior School, Sheffield

The Falcon Race Car

The Falcon V8 race car
Built in Austria
Stream-lined, cool, stylish
Like a knife slicing through cheese
It makes me feel like the king of the road
Falcon V8 race car
It's my dream to drive one.

Jack Walker (11)
Eckington Junior School, Sheffield

Summer Is . . .

The taste of beautiful cold juice
Running down my throat.
The sound of sizzling sausages on
The barbecue.
The smell of sun lotion on people's skin.
The feel of sharks swimming in the water.
The sight of the blazing red sun in the sky.

Adam James Cox (9)
Eckington Junior School, Sheffield

Summer Is . . .

The sound of the lawn mower running up and
down on the summer grass.
The taste of watery ice cream melting in my
mouth.
The touch of warm sizzling sun on my neck.
The smell of flowers swaying in the breeze.
The sight of children running around making
sandcastles.
Summer is all of these.

Rebecca Saunby (9)
Eckington Junior School, Sheffield

Summer Is . . .

The taste of sweet apples in my dry mouth.
The sight of people having fun on
the beautiful beach.
The smell of melting chocolate on my
tongue.
The touch of sand on my soft fee.
The sound of birds in the nest cheeping
for food.
Summer is . . . all of these.

Ismay Gavelle (9)
Eckington Junior School, Sheffield

Winter Haiku

Stars glitter at night
The smoke hovers in the sky
Black ice lays at night.

Sheridan Eusman (10)
Eckington Junior School, Sheffield

The Summer Is . . .

The taste is a glass of water
whetting my whistle after a match.
The sound is of children screaming
at the park sliding down the slide.
The smell of burning bangers
by the barbecue with burgers and buns.
The feel of the sun on the
back of my sunburnt neck.
The sight of the ice cream man
coming towards me.
Summer is . . . all of these.

Ashley Roberts (9)
Eckington Junior School, Sheffield

Summer Is . . .

The taste of ice cream on your tongue and the crunching
of a cornet on my teeth.
The sound of a smooth sea and ocean waves.
The smell of suntan lotion in the sun.
The feel of grass tickling my toes.
The sight of trees rustling in the breeze.

Kurt Price (9)
Eckington Junior School, Sheffield

Summer Is . . .

The taste of a cool drink trickling down my throat.
The sight of the sea and the waves blowing in the wind.
The sound of the waves rippling on the beach.
The feel of the cool water on my feet.
The smell of salt as I swim in the sea.
Summer is all of these.

Tom O'Hara (8)
Eckington Junior School, Sheffield

The Skeleton Returns

Off we go into the night
    but
it always gives me a fright
    I
thought I'd survive for one day
    and
the skeleton said, 'You are gonna pay!'

When I got up in the morning
    I
thought, *what shall I do next?*
    I
was scared, really scared
    not
that anyone cared.

It was almost night-time
    my
hair was like a mop
    I
thought I'd give the skeleton a present
such as a pair of really smelly socks.

When I heard the word bedtime
    from
my dad, I felt scared and sad
    when
I looked behind in fear, I said,
    'Please
don't eat my ears!
    Aargh!'

Hasib Afzal
Field Lane J&I School, Batley

Hair

Hair, hair everywhere
Scruffy hair, here and there
Straight hair
Curly hair
Crimped hair
Black hair
Blonde hair
Strong
Who cares?
Hair, hair, after bath
Dry it
Comb it
Brush it
Part it
Whatever, with my hair.

Aamira Pandor & Rebekah (11)
Field Lane J&I School, Batley

The Night

Just as the moon appears in the sky
I don't know why I start to cry.

It makes me remember something
I don't know what it is

Maybe it's something to do
With my mum's wedding ring.

I look back up
High in the sky
Again and again
I start to cry.

Ammaarah Chhibda
Field Lane J&I School, Batley

A Teacher Being Given Chocolate Cake

Yesterday, my worst pupil,
Had a page ripped out of his book.
He told his friends he didn't care,
But *they* didn't see the look!

Today, I got a nice, big slice,
From him, of chocolate cake.
He said that it was home-made
And took him hours to make.

It's his birthday in September
And mine is in late May.
So I really don't understand,
What's special about today.

Is it out of the goodness of his heart?
Is he being kind?
He may have planted dynamite,
Or poisonous gas inside.

Or maybe a hungry piranha,
Would like the taste of my head?
I bet this cake is dangerous,
He wants me to be dead.

There may be something I'm allergic to
Inside, like jelly or peanuts.
Or something really smelly,
Like the reek of my mate's foot.

I take a little nibble,
I take a bigger bite.
I stuff the cake inside my mouth
And it tastes alright.

I go outside and say,
'I'm sorry for being so suspicious,'
'That's all right, Miss,' he says,
'I know manure pie is delicious.'

Joanne Bailey (11)
Humberston CE Primary School, Grimsby

Oranges And Lemons

A juicy taste of an orange
And a bit of sour in a lemon
I need to get a tenner
To buy a yellow lemon.

It smells like dust
And is smelly like a skunk
It's horrible like rust
I hate oranges
They are yucky and gooey
And all juicy.

It looks like planet Jupiter
The lemon looks like Venus
They are all round
They look all yellow and orange.

It sounds all squashy
And all squidgy
And sounds like you wouldn't want to eat it.

Kieran Tynan (8)
Humberston CE Primary School, Grimsby

The River

The river meanders around the rocks
It flows and flows, it never stops
Bumping, crashing, side to side
Water splashing everywhere
Calm, slow, steady and fast
Slowly sliding down the river and tumbling into the sea.

Lucy Telford (10)
Humberston CE Primary School, Grimsby

War Ends

Loved, cherished
Jumping for joy
Seeing my kids again
Coming home to a new country
Things destroyed, houses ruined
But knowing my family is all right
Then that's all that matters
All the people out there
Lost their families and friends
I don't think war has finished
It's just started
Not seeing my son for six months
I am distraught
If you ever get asked to go to war
Say *no!*
Family is more important.

Lorna Stafford (11)
Humberston CE Primary School, Grimsby

I Am A Seed

Murky soil,
A nervous wreck.
Dingy and gloomy,
Drab and dull.
I scream because I'm scared.
I'm miserable,
It's awful.

I'm joyous,
Vivid light,
Dazzling.
Contented as I grow,
My glossy coat is cracking.
Cheerful, jovial,
I'm happy.

Matthew Bailey (9)
Humberston CE Primary School, Grimsby

Oranges

Yellow oranges sweet and round,
but they make no loud sound.
Very, very juicy in your mouth
and very, very brightly coloured.

Very plain and that really is a shame
but sometimes sweet and kind of sugary.
A smell of an orange is hard to beat
You will *drift off your feet.*

Orange-looking and very round,
Looks like eyeballs whenever found.
Yellow, orange, blue and green, very colourful,
Every year they grow even in snow.
Squirty, chewy, never hard but never, ever speak,
But I know they speak, 'Ssh,'
Or *get out of town!*

Saskia Wilbourne-Davy (7)
Humberston CE Primary School, Grimsby

The Delicious Dinner

Meat so crunchy and so yummy
I like a cooked tea from my mummy.
Sauce so runny and so delicious
Tomato very splatty and so tasty.

Smell those delicious peppers in the air
So I run downstairs, tomato with peppers, so scrumptious.
I have to get it down me, it makes me so hungry
I just gobble it all down.

I see the scrumptious leaves
With the delicious chicken
And the tasty roll with the spicy peppers
With the bumpy bread.

Joshua Winchester (7)
Humberston CE Primary School, Grimsby

Food Poem

The white flour like snow,
The long string like a tangled worm.
Red cherries like a red nose,
An orange looks like sweet honey.

I like the smell of chocolate mix burning,
Apricots smell like fresh trees.
Nuts smell like cornflakes out of the packet,
Oranges smell like fresh fruit.

I can see flowers falling like rain,
The cake looks delicious.
The jelly looks like gold in a treasure chest,
The orange looks like golden honey, it's runny.

I can hear the bowl rattling in the cupboard,
The caterpillar creeping on the wall.
A piece of paper crinkling,
I can hear rain going *pitter-patter*.

Bethany Mae Stanham (8)
Humberston CE Primary School, Grimsby

My Back Garden

I can hear the birds singing in the bushes
People chatting as they walk past
There is water dancing on my holly tree
I can hear the bushes, *rustling* bushes
Creaking, bedroom window going *spook*
All of my plants are singing with a *swoosh*.

Big bumblebees buzzing round my head
I have a grid and when people walk past, it goes *bump*
My pavement is going *pitter-patter* as people ride past
I can hear people driving *speedily* past in the morning.

Samuel Cavendish (8)
Humberston CE Primary School, Grimsby

Seed Poem

I am a seed.
I feel guarded.
But sometimes scared.
My shell protects me.
I feel solitary also.
I am trying to break through.
I'm cold, wet, moist.
It's damp and squirmy.

Finally, I'm busting through.
I feel not unlit.
Not too saturated.
Very unfamiliar, but lovely.
I feel warm, not cold.
I feel rain on top of me.
My leaves begin to spurt out of me.
I feel free and ready to flower.

Max Allen (8)
Humberston CE Primary School, Grimsby

Small Ad!

1990s brother.
Very reliable but
tends to slow down
after two miles!

Not as big
as it could be
but perfect for two!

Comes in a variety
of colours including
brown, green and red!

Would exchange
for a more sporty edition!

Rosie Murphy (11)
Humberston CE Primary School, Grimsby

Delicious Food

The yummy, delicious olives, waiting to be eaten
And the horrid nuts I hate to eat
The crunchy tomatoes taste like feet
I leave them on my plate, nice and neat
I smell the delicious frying in the pan on a Sunday morning
On Christmas morning, the turkey sizzling in the oven
When I have cheese on toast
I see the cheese melt on it
It looks like blood coming out my knee.

Joseph Robinson (8)
Humberston CE Primary School, Grimsby

Cornwall Beach

I hear the twisting waves in the sea
And the sand, swirling on the ground.
I like to hear the rocks in the streams rocking about
And the stream swirling around them.
I can hear the fences creaking in the wind
And bursting down the hills.
I can imagine the rocks creaking in the caves.

Emma De Halle (8)
Humberston CE Primary School, Grimsby

Classroom

It makes you dizzy when everyone speaks at once.
When everyone moves their chair, it squeaks and squeaks everywhere.
When everyone stamps their feet it sounds like a bear roaring.
Some people have heels and go *flip-flop* and it is a racket.
When people open their tray it sounds like sandpaper.

Georgia Strong (8)
Humberston CE Primary School, Grimsby

Pleasure Island

I hear the noisy rides *scraping* on the ground
I like to hear birds tweeting like a whistle
When rides are *whooshing* through the air
The people start screaming on the *spooky* ride
I like it when I hear horses *clattering* at Pleasure Island
Everything is noisy because my ears go *plop*
Then *splash* I'm in the water boat and down the slide
That what I can hear
Pleasure Island is fun!

Sydney Hutchison (7)
Humberston CE Primary School, Grimsby

Beach

Clattering bucket and spade.
Children laughing and playing.
Loud waves smashing on the rocks.
Children running in the muddy water.
Swirling waves softly splashing on the waves.
Smashing waves on a deep rock.

Paige Stafford (8)
Humberston CE Primary School, Grimsby

Pleasure Island

I hear the rushing boomerang
The people screaming as it moves around
The slide is scratching in the breeze
It hurts my ear, it's squeaking down
I hear babies screaming on the Froggie.

Lucy Stables (8)
Humberston CE Primary School, Grimsby

The Changing Moon

One, two, three, look up at me,
One, two, three, I'm way above the trees.

The full moon is like an icy snowball
being tossed into never-ending darkness,
like a silver coin, disappearing in the big, black till,
like a speeding bullet, being shot into a black hole.

One, two, three, look up at me,
One, two, three, I'm way above the trees.

The crescent moon is like a sabre fang
slicing through the dark sky,
like a white boomerang, whizzing through the bright stars,
like a small hammock, carefully suspending the night sky.

One, two, three, look up at me,
One, two, three, I'm way above the trees.

Jacob Gabbitas (9)
Humberston CE Primary School, Grimsby

The Changing Moon

The full moon is like a crystal ball telling your future,
Like a big tennis ball being batted into space,
Like a white lollipop on an invisible stick.

Look up high in the night,
You'll see something shining bright.

The crescent moon is like a bull's horn in the dusky sky,
Like an ear on an invisible face
Like a puzzled looking eyebrow.

Look up high in the night,
You'll see something shining bright.

Alice Epton (9)
Humberston CE Primary School, Grimsby

My Seed

I am alone, scared, lonely
But a bit frightened
I am waiting for something to happen.
Wet, damp, want to get out of this rusty coating.
That looks unfamiliar
It's the . . . sun
I am tingling, magnificent
I am growing
It's beautiful.
This is the best day of my life
I am happy.
This is so great
Oh my, flowers have appeared.
It's raining again
I am so happy.

Steffan Puckey (9)
Humberston CE Primary School, Grimsby

Blitzed

Nice and cosy in my bed,
Then the siren goes.
All of a sudden bombs dropping,
Bang! Bang! I hear.

I run like a cheetah to my shelter,
I feel horrified and scared.
Come back out, everything blown up,
Hot as the sun the fire spreads.

Happy not to die yet,
Rescued by wardens.
Firefighters everywhere,
Goodbye to other people.

Daniel Fisher (11)
Humberston CE Primary School, Grimsby

Hope

Yellow is the colour of hope
Ripe grapes is the taste of hope
Hope smells like the sweetest flower
Chirping birds in the morning
Is the sound of hope
Warm, fluffy pillows
Is the feel of hope
Hope lives in everyone.

Emily Stanham (10)
Humberston CE Primary School, Grimsby

Love

Love is the colour of the reddest roses,
It smells like the fresh breeze,
Love tastes like smooth chocolate,
The sound of wedding bells,
It feels like sugar rolling in your mouth,
It lives in people's bodies.

Charlotte Robinson (10)
Humberston CE Primary School, Grimsby

Pain

Pain is the colour of the darkest night,
It smells like dog's droppings,
Pain tastes like the most mouldy apple,
It sounds like girls screaming,
It feels like the sharpest knife,
Pain lives in the darkest cave.

Michael Hutchison (10)
Humberston CE Primary School, Grimsby

Hope

Hope is the colour of lush grass,
It smells like the spray of haze
And tastes like fresh water,
Hope sounds like the chirping of the first bird of dawn,
It feels like smooth chocolate,
Hope lives deep inside your loving heart.

Billy King (9)
Humberston CE Primary School, Grimsby

Friendship

Friendship is yellow
Smells like summer daffodils
It tastes like candy
Friendship sounds quiet
It feels like a rose petal
Friendship lives in your heart!

Lindsey Todd (10)
Humberston CE Primary School, Grimsby

Hope

Hope is the colour gold,
It smells like food cooking,
Hope tastes like chocolate,
Hope sounds like the calm sea,
It feels like the wind brushing on your face,
Hope lives everywhere.

Jerome Harper (9)
Humberston CE Primary School, Grimsby

Beach

I walk on the crunching, swishing sand.
I hear the whistling, blowing wind.
I see the crashing, smashing, rushing and banging waves.
The seagulls are screaming and calling to me.
I see them dropping.
I hear them hooting.
The waves look like dolphins coming to me.

Faye Costello (8)
Humberston CE Primary School, Grimsby

Peace

Peace is the colour of sky blue,
It smells like fresh flowers,
It tastes like summer fruits,
Peace sounds like singing birds,
It feels like the warm sun is shining,
Peace lives in your heart.

Alice Downes (9)
Humberston CE Primary School, Grimsby

Hope

It's gleaming gold,
It smells like fresh flowers,
Hope tastes like sweet potatoes,
Hope's the sound of a calm breeze,
It feels like being under a waterfall,
Hope lives in your whole body.

Sarah Quinn (10)
Humberston CE Primary School, Grimsby

Fairy Land

I hear fairies *twinkle* because they've just been born.
Then I like to hear *rustling* in the magic trees.
Danger! Is what I hear in the magic wood.
Whispering fairies and *screaming* that is what I hear.

Virginia Read (7)
Humberston CE Primary School, Grimsby

The Beach

The sea was splashing and the water was sploshing.
The waves were *clashing* on the rocks.
It was *smashing* and *bashing*
The wind was swirling.
The sound of music from the arcades.

Joseph Steel (8)
Humberston CE Primary School, Grimsby

Frosty Garden

I hear the crackling of the glassy ice.
I like to hear the crunching of the grass.
I listen to the falling snowflakes.
I hear the smashing of the snowballs.

Louis Townell (8)
Humberston CE Primary School, Grimsby

Swimming Pool

I hear the splashing in the pool,
The laughter and the fun, the singing and the joyful day,
The people calling to one another,
Today is a sunny day, people jumping off the bouncing diving board,
Screeching children all around.

Sophie Goldsmith (7)
Humberston CE Primary School, Grimsby

Hate

Hate is the colour of smokey-black
It smells like mouldy, rotted, old bins
Hate sounds like the howling of werewolves
When the moon comes out in the middle of the night
Hate tastes like big chunks of soil
Hate feels like falling over on the gritty pavement
Hate lives under the ground.

Lauren Costello (10)
Humberston CE Primary School, Grimsby

Friendship

Friendship is the colour of red,
It smells like hot cocoa,
Sweetest sugar.
It sounds like laughing,
It feels warm from head to toe,
Friendship lives in the heart.

Emma Winn (10)
Humberston CE Primary School, Grimsby

Pain

Pain is the colour of the darkest black.
It smells like rotted bodies.
Pain tastes like the blood from a dead shark.
It sounds like a lion getting stabbed.
It feels like a dinosaur lashing at you.
Pain lives in every cold-hearted person.

George Baker (10)
Humberston CE Primary School, Grimsby

Grandad

Grey and black straight hair,
Blue, sapphire eyes smiling at me,
Sleeping silently, sometimes horrid, loud, banging and shouting.
Soft wrinkly hands, curling in my fingers,
Red, rosy lips touching my silky lips.
I'm sad and miserable, sorrowful and gloomy,
I taste the salty sea fish he loved to cook,
I smell the raw fish straight from the sea.

Bethaney Nicolson (9)
Humberston CE Primary School, Grimsby

Death

Death is a deep blood-red,
It smells like rotten flesh.
Death tastes like mouldy bread,
It sounds like fingernails scratching at a chalky blackboard.
The feel of death is like a blunt knife
Cutting slowly through your heart.
It lives at the bottom of your grave.

Holly Mavin (10)
Humberston CE Primary School, Grimsby

Cruelty

Cruelty is the colour of fresh, red blood
It smells like spilled gas
The taste is like a mouldy apple
It sounds like the wind howling on a bad night
The cruelty makes you feel pain all over
It lives in the middle of the sharpest knife.

Hannah Taylor (9)
Humberston CE Primary School, Grimsby

Goodbye

Silent, sad, scared
Terrified with tears dripping
Petrified, in pain and anger
Distraught with fear and wondering
Miserable, reluctant
Confused, but heartbroken
Destroyed with pain and fear
Feeling unloved and punished
While I love and hug him, nervous and cold
Will he ever come back?

Danielle Gilchrist (11)
Humberston CE Primary School, Grimsby

On The Cliff Top

Flying, flying up high
Whilst being in the sky
Little did Icarus know
He was about to die!

While he was flying
Up high in the sky
Splat! Dead
From up high in the sky.

Ellis Daniel Mortimore (11)
Humberston CE Primary School, Grimsby

A Teacher's View Of Being Given Cake

Today I was given a piece of cake,
By somebody I really hate.
What's his plan? What's his trick?
Cake from a boy called Nasty Nick.
Why's it green and yellow too?
Do you think . . . ? I do!

James Holliday (11)
Humberston CE Primary School, Grimsby

Flying High - Icarus And Daedal

Standing on top of a mountain, terrified
'We must set off quickly,' my father said
The sun is shining, the sky is blue
How these wings are going to work, I don't have a clue
Suddenly, I pushed off, flying in the air
I'm disobeying my father, but I don't care.

'Stop, Icarus, you're flying too high
High into the big blue sky.
The wax shall melt with the heat of the sun
This is no time for fun'
But it's too late and Icarus is dead.

Monketh Jaibaji (10)
Humberston CE Primary School, Grimsby

Dinosaur

D estroying dinosaurs are my favourite animals
I nconsiderate of animals smaller than themselves
N ot scared of anything, even death
O nly tortoises still live from that time
S ome dinosaurs were as tall as a skyscraper
A ll dinosaurs are now not alive
U nfriendly you wouldn't be mates with these
R eptile is their type.

Daniel Lond (11)
Humberston CE Primary School, Grimsby

Snake Poem

S lithering along the dry ground
N earer to its prey
A ttacking the animal with its venom-drenched fangs
K nocked out the small bird
E vil in the snake's eyes, he eats it whole
S atisfied snake sneaks off for its next meal.

Stephen Ashton (11)
Humberston CE Primary School, Grimsby

The Teacher's Cake

Today I was given some cake,
I opened it at break,
The white, whipped cream,
Seemed to have a little hint of green,
Was it poison
Or was it clean?
Could it kill,
Or was it safe?
He had a little grin on his face,
Could it kill? It's a case!

Karl Evardson (11)
Humberston CE Primary School, Grimsby

Goodbye

I'm silent, sad and shocked by my fears.
Petrified with pain in my stomach.
Hungry and thirsty with nothing to do.
Lonely and lost I don't know where I'm going.
Cold and heartbroken.
Agitated and angry and lost with fears.
Puzzled and depressed with my gas mask.
Shocked and bewildered with the darkness.

Daniel Parker (11)
Humberston CE Primary School, Grimsby

Friendship

Friendship is the colour of red
It smells of blooming flowers
It tastes of strawberry lipsyl
It sounds like a kitten purring
It feels good and great
It lives in my heart in me.

Paige Fenwick (9)
Humberston CE Primary School, Grimsby

Wisdom

Shall I open the door,
Or close the door?
I am so confused!
I have just one question though.

Do I have wisdom?
Does she and he have wisdom?
Does everyone have wisdom?

Then a brainwave came to mind,
Of course, we *all* have *wisdom!*

Nicola Bell (11)
Humberston CE Primary School, Grimsby

Cake Dilemma

Is it full of poison
Or is it out of date?
Why has she given me this small piece of cake?
Has it been sat on
Or is it perfectly fine?
I'll only know if I have a little try.
Is it revenge on what I did last night
Or is it a yummy cake that I might like?

Emily Pullan (11)
Humberston CE Primary School, Grimsby

Love

Love is lipstick red,
It smells like spring roses,
Love tastes like sweet candy,
It sound like lipstick kissing,
It feels soft and gentle,
Love lives in your heart.

Melissa Balderson (10)
Humberston CE Primary School, Grimsby

My Cat

Greasy, smooth coat,
Deep green eyes, like swimming pools,
Rubber feet as they stick to the floor.
Wet, rosy nose, shines in the light,
Paws tapping up and down the stairs.
Ears pointed like pins,
Smells of fresh air as she prowls our garden.
Rough and wet tongue
And that is my cat.

Abigail King (8)
Humberston CE Primary School, Grimsby

Fear

Fear is the colour of darkest grey,
It smells cold and bitter.
Fear tastes rotten and mouldy,
The sound of a howl of a wolf.
It has a touch like an ice cube,
You will find it in a graveyard.

Josephine Aitchison (10)
Humberston CE Primary School, Grimsby

Hope

Hope is sky-blue.
It smells like home-made cakes.
Hope tastes like triple chocolate cookies.
It sounds like birds tweeting.
Hope feels like a soft colour.
It lives in your heart.

Daisy Gough (10)
Humberston CE Primary School, Grimsby

The Maze

The damp, dark maze,
Had a really big phase,
The Minotaur's roar,
Closed the door,
The chamber smelt stranger,
I was heading into danger,
The time had come,
The battle had begun.

My sword went *swish,*
The Minotaur went *swash,*
The sword went speeding,
He was bleeding,
Off with his head,
He was dead,
I went rushing,
He was gushing,
I went home.

David Low (11)
Humberston CE Primary School, Grimsby

Hope

Hope is the colours silver and gold.
It smells like a fresh summer's day.
Hope tastes like juicy oranges.
It sounds like fun and laughter.
Hope feels like a hot water bottle.
Hope lives in your soul.

Alex Thompson (10)
Humberston CE Primary School, Grimsby

Cheerful, Delighted, Over The Moon

I'm terrified, but excited,
I can't wait to see him again,
My mother is dancing and prancing around,
I'm trying not to make a sound.

Here he comes, down the drive,
I'm trying to hold it in,
But it's useless, oh it is,
I have to scream aloud.

I run outside and don't care
If I get mud on my socks,
'Oh father, it is, it's really you'
And I gave him a great, big hug.

Abbie Felton (11)
Humberston CE Primary School, Grimsby

A Teacher's View On Being Given Cake

Yesterday, Jack was in trouble
The work he had done was a complete muddle
He's just given me a slice of cake
Could this be a mistake?
His birthday isn't today
It's in a few months in the middle of May
Is this a peace offering
Or is it a trick?
Will this cake make me feel quite sick?
I'm taking no chances
It's going in the bin
'Now children, stop making such a din!'

Jonathan Parker (11)
Humberston CE Primary School, Grimsby

Swimming Pools

People go swimming at pools
Some people swim in the seas
Some people are just fools
For the sea will make you freeze.

The sea is full of fish
Fish dance all day long
Chuck a coin and make a wish
All day long you'll hear a song.

In a pool you can splish and splash,
In a pool it is always full
Steady on, here comes a flash
And you will find it is never dull.

In water you can do some sports
Things like water polo
Boys wear swimming shorts
You can't play polo solo.

Hannah Smith (9)
Leys Farm Junior School, Scunthorpe

Waterfall

W aterfalls splish and splash
A nd fall down like a water slide
T he clear water is very relaxing
E very day its clean water whooshes down
R efreshing water tumbles down like a pile of rocks
F alling water is never-ending
A lways crashing on the rocks
L ashing white water spraying
L ooks like a volcano erupting.

Imogen Culbert (9)
Leys Farm Junior School, Scunthorpe

Water

Most animals love water
Like dogs, mice and rats too
Do you like water too, too, too?
Do you? Do you? (like water too.)

Tell me now, if you like water
Dogs and tigers swim in water
Yes they do, yes, yes, yes
They do.

There are different types of water
Like sea water and the water
That comes out of your tap
Water, water, I love water.

Charlotte Arrand (9)
Leys Farm Junior School, Scunthorpe

Swimming Pool

S wimming slowly around in the pool
W ishy, washy waves
 I n the pool it is very warm
M oving slowly in the pool
M oving quickly and furiously
 I n the flumes you go very fast
N ever dive into the shallow end
G oing slow on the surface of the water
P ools are noisier than a car's engine revving
O ver the waves we jump
O ver the waves we splash
L ong flumes twirling and twisting.

Damien Henderson (9)
Leys Farm Junior School, Scunthorpe

Water Time

Irina looked at the waterfall
Its crashing water
Its roar of laughter
As it makes its way down.

Irina moved closer,
Put out one hand
As the water trickled down her arm
She felt the coolness of the water.

As it carries it to a little lake
It lays still
Not a muscle moving
Its voice not showing
Ripples and crashes are no more.

Irina loved the water.

Eleanor Dawson (8)
Leys Farm Junior School, Scunthorpe

Waterfalls

W ater is see-through
A t waterfalls the water slaps against the rocks
T oday I went to the waterfall
E veryday I see the beautiful white water
R ound the rocky sea bends to get there
F orever the water flows
A ll the water goes bright white when it smashes
L ong rock eroding little stones
L ong water going all the way down the waterfall
S liding down the shining rocks.

Stephen Hutchinson (8)
Leys Farm Junior School, Scunthorpe

A Water Droplet's Journey

In the sea it
Is calm and green
Where the water vapour
Lay.

While you're playing at
The beach, the vapour
Is evaporating high
In the sky.

In the cloud the millions
And billions too heavy
For the cloud then . . .

The cloud splits letting rain
Hit the floor, tap! Tap! Tap!

Some of the water hits the mountain
Forming a stream, starting the cycle all over again.

Alex Todd (9)
Leys Farm Junior School, Scunthorpe

The Sea

The sea crashes against rocks of crystal
The water waving and whirling around
Out to sea.

The sharks charging like rhinos
The squid letting out its ink at fish
Out to sea.

The pearls gleaming as white as paper
The weed and coral tough as chains
Out to sea.

Robert Peden (9)
Leys Farm Junior School, Scunthorpe

Waterfall

The splashy waterfall
Is shaped like a lacy shawl.

It runs down without any fear.
The noise of splish and splash goes through
Your ear.

It feels good
You just knew it would,
It smells clean,
The finest you've ever seen.

You'll get lots of calls,
To come and see the lovely falls
It runs down like raindrops falling
Droplets running, droplets calling
The lacy water never ends
It keeps on going round the bends.

Amelia Whiteside (9)
Leys Farm Junior School, Scunthorpe

The Stream

The stream was flowing to and fro
The stream was whistling a beautiful song
The stream was crashing against the rocks
The stream was as fast as a cheetah running
The stream was as clear blue as the sky
The water was crashing down the stream
It made me feel so relaxed.

Lewis Dawson (9)
Leys Farm Junior School, Scunthorpe

The Waterfall Of Talu River

It starts as a trickle
        Which makes your toes tickle
                Then turns into a spring
                        I wonder what next it will bring?
                Will it bring?
        I wonder what next it will bring?

A river?
A rapid?
Or a rumbling waterfall rainbow?

As it drifts along
Like a billabong
        Trees, secrets,
                Whispering breeze.

Rushing river
        Branches in a quiver
Trees blow in the breeze.

Seven streaks of light fading away
        The water sparkles like sapphires and diamonds
                Lapping over the rocks.

Like magic the moon peers out from behind
The golden outlined clouds and shines down
        And makes the water sparkle, glint, shimmer and glimmer.

Listen. Look. Peace at last
        Tiny fish dart and flip in and out of the silvery rocks . . .
Night falls . . . Stars begin to play
The cool stillness of the water drifts away
For another adventure the fish have to wait till next day.

Lauren Darn (9)
Leys Farm Junior School, Scunthorpe

The Dolphin

Underneath
The water
Animals you will see
Seals here, sharks there
Dolphins leaping out to sea
Sharks are looking for their tea
Mind out fishes!
But one moment
Splash! A dolphin saves the fish
And the shark loses the fish dish
Dolphins are very loyal
And kind to
Their seal buddies.
Dolphins are   hurt
By   sharks
So the dolphins   make the water hot
And they put   a shark in the cooking
Pot!

Jodie Flynn (10)
Leys Farm Junior School, Scunthorpe

A Poem About Water

Water pours down waterfalls back into the wild river
The splashing is as loud as Saint James' Park
When Shearer scores a goal.
The water is as quick as a hungry
Cheetah chasing a gazelle.
The water rapids are as white as a terrible blizzard
But when the water reaches the sea it's
As peaceful and calm as a fluffy cloud.

Callum Thompson (9)
Leys Farm Junior School, Scunthorpe

The Waterfall

Splishing and splashing
Swishing and crashing
Like a lion's roar
So pretty and so beautiful
You'll want to stay for more

Like shaving foam on a hand
Or a pool of blue and white
With lovely plants and lovely rants
About this water delight.

With wondrous trees
And all that sees
This wondrous waterfall.

Amy Smith (9)
Leys Farm Junior School, Scunthorpe

Rivers

Rivers are wiggly and windy
Inside rivers you can see fishes
Vanishing into the weeds
Ever seen a beautiful river
Running into the sea
Seaweed swaying from side to side?

Kirsty Grey (9)
Leys Farm Junior School, Scunthorpe

Raindrops

Raindrops from clouds
Across the sky, side by side
Inside the clouds are raindrops
Now are ready to drop to the ground.

Charlie Cross
Leys Farm Junior School, Scunthorpe

Dog's Life

A to Z of different names,
Yorkshire terriers to Great Danes,
From the hearthrug by the fire,
To their masters great desire.

It's walk time, hurry up,
You cute, little, lazy pup,
Chasing squirrels and big fat cats,
And of course our master's hats!

Dinner time! Hip, hip hooray,
We've all had a wonderful day,
I really like the master and his wife,
And as for us, it's a perfect dog's life!

Freya Bradshaw (9)
Leys Farm Junior School, Scunthorpe

The Rivers

The river is cold
The river is fast
The river clashes on the rocks
The river goes side to side
The river feels like it is talking to you.

The river smells like old fish
The river sounds like a boat going
Through the sea
The river is where fish live
The river is rain water.

Laura-Beth Ward (9)
Leys Farm Junior School, Scunthorpe

Fire At Priory Lane

When I walked into the school I saw a
Kitchen full of dinner ladies sitting on chairs and putting food on
Our plates and setting out chairs to sit on.
A place to have assemblies to share our thoughts
To sing, to give awards to people for doing
Something good, to find out what people
Do for a living, to have discos, performances, celebrations
There we all had fun.

But this was before the fire.

Now we cannot gather as a school to do drama
Or fun PE lessons like we used to have.
We cannot drink the tap water because it is
Contaminated by black sparks of dust.
Now as I look into the school hall I see
Ruins of the piano and the mats all torn apart
Everyone was shocked as this was happening.

When our school is finished it will be the best hall ever
It will look great with brand new footballs and stuff for PE
And everything will be brilliant.

Kellie Martin (10)
Priory Lane Junior School, Scunthorpe

My Great Dog

My beautiful dog Casper
Is simply the best
Even though he can be a bit of a pest.
Those big brown eyes; that wet, shiny nose,
You should see how fast he goes.

Elizabeth Orwin (9)
Priory Lane Junior School, Scunthorpe

Untitled

The school hall used to have
Crystal clear windows
And lovely displays
On the colourful boards
It used to have such a fresh clean smell
Like fresh morning air
When I walked into the hall
I felt warm and safe inside
I smelt fresh food
Served out to all the children
I heard children talking and laughing

The school hall now has dirty smelly floors and black walls
It has no roof and it is looking at the sky above
The kitchen is burnt like a crispy turkey
I feel sad and angry at the same time
No more crystal clear windows but
Dirty smelly walls and shattered window frames
On the floor like an abandoned junk pile.

Jessica Johnston (10)
Priory Lane Junior School, Scunthorpe

At The Seaside

At the seaside
I like to play
In the sand.

At the seaside
I like to catch fishes
And play in the sea.

At the seaside
I like to fly my kite
And watch as it blows
In the sky.

Emily Mee (8)
Priory Lane Junior School, Scunthorpe

The Attack Of The Arsonist(s)

I walked through the hall doors and I saw
A hall as homely as your bed
The sweet scent of cleanliness, just after the hall had been cleaned
The celebrations of Halloween, Valentine's Day and assemblies
This is what the school used to have

Now with the school hall ruined I saw
The stripped patchwork wall
The swinging collapsed roof of steel
The melted double doors, bent as if it were paper
The tables and chairs rusted as if they had been left out for 25 years
I felt unsafe, very unsafe

In the future they might be
A comfy padded floor, as comfy as a cloud
New PE equipment as gleaming as a piece of polished glass
Crystal clear water pouring out the tap
This is what the school might have
Now I feel safe.

Cameron Lee (9)
Priory Lane Junior School, Scunthorpe

The Sunflower

Sunflower shine as bright as the sun.
The green soft leaves reach up.
High, high to the big, blue sky.
The roots stretch like wiggly toes.

The soft green stem
Reaches, high, high.
For the sunflower.

The plant pots are brown
Like melted chocolate
The soft earth around the plant
Protects it like a blanket in a baby's cot.

Jessica Wheeler (8)
Priory Lane Junior School, Scunthorpe

At The Seaside

At the seaside
I like to play games
And ride donkeys.

At the seaside
I like to find shells
And dig in the sand.

At the seaside
I like to make sandcastles
And bury my friends.

At the seaside
I like to swim
And play in the sea.

Olivia Paige Graves (7)
Priory Lane Junior School, Scunthorpe

The Magic Box

(Based on 'Magic Box' by Kit Wright)

In my magic box I will put . . .
A half of a fairy's wing
The first man to drink whisky
A whale's big mouldy teeth
A mammoth's shiny tusk
A baby's first cute smile.

In my magic box I will put . . .
A dog's short, stumpy tail
A pig's big, veiny ear
The first caveman's stick
The first man to talk in history
A magic, talking, golden tree.

Harry Pask (9)
Priory Lane Junior School, Scunthorpe

I Will Put In My Box

(Based on 'Magic Box' by Kit Wright)

I will put in my box . . .
The brightest sun and the bluest sky.
The smell of a rich lady's perfume
And the five senses that we have.

I will put in my box . . .
A fierce dragon's breath so hot.
Every achievement ever to be achieved
A pony's long golden mane.

I will put in my box . . .
A cheetah's black spots
An owl's curved beak
And finally the fish that swim in the blue ocean.

I will put in my box . . .
The flash of a dolphin's eye
The sound of the gallop of a horse
The flapping wings of a bird in the sun.

My box is painted gold
It has the shiniest, silver star on the top
It glitters like a rainbow in the sun
And when you look inside you can see every colour in the world.

Katy Harrison (9)
Priory Lane Junior School, Scunthorpe

Best Friends

Best friends should always be there
To love each other and care
To help one another
Also sisters and brothers
To share secrets forever
And always be together.

Abigail Corsair (8)
Priory Lane Junior School, Scunthor pe

The Colour Collation

Yellow, red, orange and green
Colours like these are the brightest I've seen.

Black, grey, blue and brown
Are dullest colours throughout the town.

But all colours are beautiful
No matter how they are.

Red, yellow or purple
Or the colours of your car.

But what is your favourite?
What is your opinion?

Well find out very soon
At the colour collation.

Rachel Wilson (10)
Priory Lane Junior School, Scunthorpe

To Mrs Clark

Mrs Clark, you are the best,
I wonder if you've had a test.
It is your best feature,
To be the greatest teacher.
I know you're really kind
And you do just have to mind.

You do things that are fun,
And sometimes give a sum.
I love to do my art,
Where everyone gets a part.
You're here and you're there,
But I'll tell them not to stare.

Nikki Koudis (9)
Priory Lane Junior School, Scunthorpe

The Consequences

As I walked through the hall doors I saw . . .
The dinner ladies busily hurrying about
Preparing a wonderful dinner
As if they were trying to feed the world.
Children running and dancing like
Dolphins in the dark, delightful sea.
Hearing the bell ringing,
Standing like statues
Rushing like cheetahs to the dinner line.

As I opened the hall doors I saw . . .
A burnt up dumping ground
Smothered with smoke and dust.
The CD player with a tape
Left dangling in the wreckage
Huge piles of dust where the
End was unseeable
I felt sad and shocked
As if my best friend was dead
The surprise gripped me and shook
Me like a tattered, old, ancient rug.
No colour,
No light,
No hall at all.

As I opened the hall doors I saw . . .
A wonderful kitchen shining
Like a glistening winter's pond.
Where there was once just plain sky
I now see the ceiling
Hanging like a canopy over me
Children waiting for an assembly in
Their *own* hall,
Some sneaky boys plonking the piano keys
And smoke alarms dotted
Everywhere like spots on a ladybird

Brilliantly coloured walls showing
Light,
Bright,
Excellent displays.
Our hall is back again!

Meadow O'Connor (10)
Priory Lane Junior School, Scunthorpe

The School Hall

My memories of the school are . . .
The peaceful sounds of the birds chirping
The wonderful noise from Mrs Potter playing her piano
The light from the sun, gleaming through the windows,
The mopped, shiny floor
The smiling faces of my friends singing,
The yummy food served by the dinner ladies,
The shiny, red card held up by Mrs Barber to stop us talking.

Now all I see is . . .
4AE's stairs being blocked off
We have no projector to help us sing
The words to our wonderful songs
Year 5 have to go round to Year 3 to get the register
We have to have our dinners at Tomo's
Pack ups have to be eaten in Year 3 area.

In the future I hope to see . . .
A gleaming kitchen, as shiny as gold
The wonderful smell of mashed potatoes on my plate
The smiling faces of dinner ladies
The pupils back together again.

Danielle Wilson (10)
Priory Lane Junior School, Scunthorpe

Our School

I walked through the doors and saw a cheerful hall decorated with
different colours,
Children drinking crystal clear water,
We sang together as one school and prayed to God,
The school had a homely smell circling its environment,
Classes having well equipped PE lessons,
Children feel safe walking around the school.
The school celebrating together and singing along to Mrs Potter's
tuneful piano,
Everything would go to plan and all the children would know where
they should be.

I am walking through the hall doors and I see
A pile of rubbish with no end,
Friends being evacuated from one place to another,
Children worrying if it is safe in the school,
Scared and sad expressions running from one face to the next,
Teachers' fighting the devastation that has happened,
A smell that surrounds the school environment,
Walls stripped by fire and one wall collapsed,
A hall with no joy, no happiness and no cheerfulness.

I will walk through the hall doors and see
Walls decorated with cheery colours,
A glistening climbing frame with a mat as soft as lamb's fur,
A giant fan to keep us cool as snowmen,
Friends with faces of joy and happiness,
Teachers glad that everything will go to plan,
Dinner ladies happy to have their kitchen back again,
Children practicing a play on a sparkling new stage,
A school full of happy faces,
Everyone is happy to have their school back to normal.

Jessica Corsair (10)
Priory Lane Junior School, Scunthorpe

The School Hall

As I glanced at the school hall I saw . . .
The same colourful decorations,
I smelt the same sweet smell like always
I saw the projector with the hymns stacked up high
The dinner ladies getting the tables and chairs ready
The children smelling lovely dinner smells and wanting their dinner
now!
The school hall floorboards shining, sparkling in the sunshine.

As I stared at the school hall I see . . .
The roof fallen in, dangling from the weak building
Tapes trailing out of the tape player,
Burnt out mats; Velcro hanging off.
The horrible sooty smell, not the usual sweet smell.
My face dropped in sadness
I saw the burnt wooden hatch,
The piano must have been burnt as well
Shattered glass lay everywhere from the glass doors
All over the floor.
Floorboards broken and sticking out
And pipes poking out of the wall in a most dangerous way.

As my eyes wondered at the new school hall I saw . . .
A spanking new CD player that
Doesn't shoot out tapes like the old one.
Worktops in the kitchen
As shiny as a mirror when it's been polished
More table and chairs as stable as a stable full of ponies
New PE equipment that's as shiny
As the hoof of horses when polished
And colourful decorations that children will love.

Jessica Shaw (10)
Priory Lane Junior School, Scunthorpe

School Hall

The school hall used to have a shiny floor,
But not anymore.
The school hall had beautifully painted walls
But not any more
Mrs Potter plonking away on the piano
But not anymore.
Why! Why! Why!
Did they have to do this?
Took our fun and laughs away from us.

But now that it is like dust, dirt and metal
With extremely sharp edges.
Thick dust, coal dust like the black sky at night
Apparatus burnt, scolded, melted.
Mats not blue like a sunny day, but burnt black.

As I stared at the school hall
Tears slowly drifting down my cheek,
My mouth wide open it was more than I had ever
Dreamed of
Shiny triple glazed windows
Built in crystal clock
50-inch 3D screen
Built in projector
Laminate flooring, shiny as a tile that you can see your face in
And spotlights on the walls so that plays can be seen
Massive chandelier dangling from the ceiling
The dinner ladies plonking lovely food on my plate
Children chomping food loudly.

Joe Toplass (10)
Priory Lane Junior School, Scunthorpe

The Burnt Down School

As I walked through the school doors I saw
A kitchen as sparkly as a diamond
Windows gleaming with sunlight
Walls as bright as the rainbow
An everlasting smell of the chocolate pudding being served
With gym equipment in the corners
And spongy red cushions on top
Mrs Potter clunking on the piano
And the sound of the children singing
The lost property box full to the rim

As I stared at the school hall I saw
The sooty black hall floors and a smoky smell
I feel sad, angry and unsafe
The school hall used to be full
Of the sound of children munching on food
Now only the sound of the falling clattering roof
Is stared at a hall
Now a deserted junkyard
A total tip with burnt walls
That used to have brightly coloured displays
Only the red and black bricks peep through
A toasted hall without butter!
It is an endless space waiting to be filled
With children's laughter once again!

My first look at the new school hall I shall see
A blue rubber hall floor
A wide screen TV playing our favourite films
The dinner ladies cooking fish and chips
And knives and forks sparkling from the sunlight's rays.

Hannah Spouge (9)
Priory Lane Junior School, Scunthorpe

I Walked Through The Hall Doors And I Saw . . .

I walked through the hall doors and I saw . . .
The school clean and shiny as a brand new car
Warm and inviting with a safe feeling like a second home
Dinner ladies putting delicious, scrumptious food on my plate
The hall smelt fresh as an air freshener
Social-fun, lots of activities-meeting place-celebrations

I walked through the make-shift doors of the school hall
The hall now as black as the ace of spades
Charred wood, crisp and flaky
Accommodating chairs are now rusty, bent, redundant
Walls as black as oil
Feeling cheated because I couldn't go to school
I was devastated, petrified because I didn't feel safe

As I walked through the shiny doors I see
A new kitchen as sparkly as a diamond
Daredevil children will once again
Mountaineer up adventurous climbing frames
Walls as colourful as the rainbow
A new sports floor, springy like a trampoline
Tables that were once rusty from the fire will
Now be shiny, clean and new
Children's laughter as they have their
Dinner in their new hall.

Jack Bower (10)
Priory Lane Junior School, Scunthorpe

Double Figures

Double figures means being ten
Owning a mobile and making a den!
Out on your own, staying out late
In the town or theme park with your new date
Looking after your younger brother
And getting told off by your mother!
Going to cinema, watching TV
Doing homework and taking responsibility
Growing taller and becoming mature
Your younger days may seem a blur
Hobbies, hobbies what do you do?
Do you hang around with your crew?
Do you mess around on a computer?
Or scoot around on a scooter?
Do you own any pets?
Has your pony won many rosettes?
All those bangles, necklaces and earrings
Brothers and sisters and interfering
Pleasure Island and all those places
Let you in now with new smiling faces
You're taller, older, they'll let you in
They now know your age is genuine
Growing up with all the fears
It'll all change in the next few years.

Meadow O'Connor (10) & Jessica Shaw (9)
Priory Lane Junior School, Scunthorpe

The Consequences Of The Arsonists

I walked through the hall doors
And saw a perfectly polished floor
Chairs and tables being put out
The smell of dinners wafting through the air,
Delightful decorations dangling all around me.
A kitchen as sparkly as the moon,
Children laughing, talking, eating, munching, chomping
Dinner ladies smiling as they dish out food
Everybody as happy as a child at the circus
The same colourful walls as beautiful as a rainbow
The school hall used to have these.

I walk through the school hall doors now and I see:
Rubble spread over a blackened floor,
No walls,
No piano,
Nothing.
The blue sky, for there is no roof,
Everything is in a heap
It looks like a giant has stood on it
Mess, mess, mess everywhere
That is what the hall is now.

When I walk into the new school hall I might see
A 48 inch TV screen
An excellent floor with padding for gymnastics,
Better decorations with colours as bright as the shiny sun
A CD player without the crackles and clicks
Fabulous equipment and PE once again inside
Everybody as happy as they used to be
That is what I hope the hall has.

Hannah Lavin (10)
Priory Lane Junior School, Scunthorpe

Priory Lane Fire

I walked noisily as usual into the old school hall, I saw
The shimmering disco lights shining down on me
The shiny, creaking floorboards that slid beneath my feet
Children laughing and having fun when it's indoor PE
Some naughty boys are standing up and smirking at their friends
Mr Ella is conducting the choir cheerfully, oh what a racket!
Oh, look at Mrs Couch's dog, she's brought it in to show,
That's what the hall used to have.

Now I peer round the boarded up doors to find that there is
Rubble piled as high as my mucky washing,
And the floor marbled with smoky dust and burnt up wood,
Ploppy puddles rest in dishes that survived
The CD player burnt and tattered
The black textured mats now in ruins,
The smiling faces of the children empty in sadness
This is what the hall is like now.

Hopefully I will look round the new hall doors and see
A fancy wooden floor polished and clean
A 44-inch screen TV blasting with sound
Colours splodged everywhere as if I walked onto a rainbow
And new blobbing, blinking blinds!
The laugh of children drifting in
And the sweet scent of dinners from the shiny kitchen
The hall is back again!

Hannah Turner (9)
Priory Lane Junior School, Scunthorpe

The Fire

The school hall used to have
Nice bright colourful walls
A PE cupboard without a door
Equipment like rounder bats and
Footballs
Dinner ladies plonking
Food on your plate
Children laughing with joy
Mrs Potter pounding the
Piano
Dinner ladies telling the
Year three's where to go after their lunch.

After the fire the whole school
Was afraid that it would happen
Again.
The school hall now has a black
Floor with bubbled varnish
There is crippled plastic on the floor
Charcoal lay there like a dead duck
That hasn't eaten for days.
There is tangled wire from the lights.

In the future the school should have
CCTV cameras
A new PE cupboard with more
Equipment in it.
A new climbing frame on the wall
With foam padded around the bars.
New tables and chairs all surrounded
By big wooden boards that are painted
A colourful dark blue.
There could be a larger kitchen and a
Larger hall.
There could be a larger TV.

Scott Strong (9)
Priory Lane Junior School, Scunthorpe

The School Hall

The school hall used to have
A sweet smell
Gently flowing its way
Through the colourful painted wall.
Like a plughole sucking down every drop of water.
It was a happy place
With people singing along with Mrs Potter
Gently playing the little old piano.
The hall used to have discos playing
Rock and Roll all night as a dog barking at a cat.
We had harvest festivals
With people bringing food for the needy.

The school has
A patchwork wall
Burnt up like crispy, old turkey.
A burnt door, with its ashes spread al across
The collapsed roof
The roof is devastated
On the bubbled varnish of the wooden floor.
The rusty old tables and chairs
Bent and battered because
Of the heat of the fire and
The 5 hours of water
Spat out of the hosepipe
Like a bullet out of a gun.

The school hall might have
A softer floor with a
Fire proof door
Modern lighting as
Bright as lightening
A bright colourful wall instead of a
Rusty old hall
Now we are together hopefully
It will be like that forever.

Paul Smith (9)
Priory Lane Junior School, Scunthorpe

The School Hall Used To Have . . .

The school hall used to have . . .
A sparkling dinner hall filled with
Children's happy laughter.

    Dinner ladies setting out clean tables and chairs,
    And dishing out delicious food,
    Sounds of children playing ball games outside,
    Now I can hear the dinner ladies biking off home
    And chatting and laughing,
    The sound of Mrs Potter playing on the piano.

The school hall now has . . .
No dinner ladies cooking delicious food for everyone.

    No lovely PE equipment to play with
    No Year 6's and no Year 3's to play with in the playground,
    No tables and chairs to sit on for lunch,
    No colour only black and grey,
    No clean hall floor for everyone,
    No roof for the old school hall.

The school hall will have . . .
A shiny new hall,

    A new hall floor to keep us safe,
    A safer roof for a safer hall,
    A bigger television for us all,
    A new climbing frame for PE
    A bigger and better kitchen to cook us nice meals,
    Great! A brand new hall, bright, shiny and new,
    Something good came out of it after all.

Matthew Kenyon (9)
Priory Lane Junior School, Scunthorpe

The School Hall

The school used to have
A gleaming shiny wooden floor
New double glazed windows with dull plastic frames
The school used to have
The sound of children in assembly
The smell of the dinners cooking
The sounds of children dancing in the hall
The school smelt as fresh as flowers

The school hall is now
As black as the ace of spades
Walls as dull as oil
Charred wood, crispy and flaky
Chairs that were once accommodating are now rust, bent and
redundant
It is now a smoky, burnt, barren wasteland
Devastated, petrified and unsafe

My hope for the school hall is
A new kitchen as shiny as diamonds
Tables bright as the gleaming sun
The walls bright as a rainbow
New PE equipment waiting for adventurous children
The school hall will be once again reunited with the children.

William Green (10)
Priory Lane Junior School, Scunthorpe

The School Hall

My memories of the school hall were
The floor clean as silver
And the smell of perfume
The hall as safe as my home
Water, clean as crystals
Dinner ladies dishing out delicious food
Disco fever all around me

As I walked through the ashes of the hall I saw
A total disaster with a horrid smell
A pile of junk and rubble with no end
The first time I have seen a barren wasteland
There once was the sounds of
Children muttering, eating food
Now only the sound of the roof clattering in the wind

My hopes for the new school hall are
A shining new hall floor
A massive new TV
Walls colourful as a rainbow, as bright as the sun
New PE equipment, ready for the children
These are my hopes for the school.

Ryan Prosser (10)
Priory Lane Junior School, Scunthorpe

Stars

Stars, stars everywhere
Twirling, twirling in the air

Flying, flying through the sky
Glittering, glittering low and high

In the night you can see
All of the twinkling stars
Just like me.

Helesha Thompson (10)
Rosehill Junior School, Rotherham

Seasons

Spring:
Getting warmer getting rid of your chill
Flowers start to grow

Summer:
Sun comes out to give you a tan
Ooh eh , such hot weather
Nobody lasts forever in this weather
Go to cool off in a cool, cool pond

Autumn:
Leaves, leaves falling off trees
Dropping to the ground
Blowing with misty wind *ooh* goes the wind

Winter:
Brrr, brrr, freezing cold
Wrap up warm, keep warm
Chilly, chilly, bitterly, bitterly
It's nippy weather.

Racheal Dobson (10)
Rosehill Junior School, Rotherham

Pets!

Today I'm going to the pet shop
I might find a white bunny that hops
I might find a dog that chases a log
Pets, pets what shall I get?
If I get a rabbit I will need some straw
So every week I'll have to buy some more
Pets, pets what shall I get?
If I get a horse
I will take it on a riding course
Pets, pets what shall I get?
If I get a rat
I will pat it on the back

Jodie Ackerman (10)
Rosehill Junior School, Rotherham

Celebs

Peter and Katy/Jordan
They still dating?
Ant and Dec
Get 'em out of here
Or on a Saturday night take them away
Will Young and Gareth Gates hand out plates
Knives and forks
Chicken or pork?
Here in the celeb world Katy Melua's hair curled
Sarah Whatmore, what more could you ask for?
Kylie and Danny or Mary-Kate and Ashley
                    Heartbroken
Silent act so old, oh have you spoken?
Negative Michael Jackson
Positive Janet Jackson
Avril Lavigne, Busted, Westlife and kitten's grandmas
Knitted them all mittens
I love celebs
Cool next-door neighbour Debbs
Oh celebs.

Chelsea Waldby (9)
Rosehill Junior School, Rotherham

Don't Mess About In The Swimming Baths

Don't mess about in the swimming baths
You will slip into the pool
Don't mess about in the swimming baths
You will just bang your head
Don't mess about in the swimming baths
You will get in trouble
Don't mess about in swimming baths
You will drown!
Mess about in the swimming baths
And someone will save you.

Ryan Gary Oxley (10)
Rosehill Junior School, Rotherham

My Mum's Shopping List

My mum's shopping list
Slimy snails
Gruesome grot
Snotty slugs
Mum why that?
Fishy guts
Gruesome slime
Snotty blood from a cat
Cockroaches body
Apples with worms in
Hair of a dog
Frogs foot, very bony
Eyes of newts
And fishy snake guts
Mum why that
Yucky dogs skin
And finally gruesome human blood soup

PS that is the most gruesome stuff my mum gets
That is the stuff that witches get
So my mum is one
The food is good though.

Christopher Niel Smith (9)
Rosehill Junior School, Rotherham

Different Weathers

The wind is a roaring lion
Biting your cheeks as it zooms past you
The rain is like a giant shower
Filling up the seas and oceans.
The thunder is an elephant stomping its heavy feet
The sun is like a phoenix flying down
Pecking us with its hot beak
And giving us sunburn
The snow is like a pack of flies
Coming down to the ground.

Kyle Pitt (10)
Rosehill Junior School, Rotherham

Pop Stars

Singing all day
Singing all night
Just have a break to have a sip of Sprite
Pop stars really are the best
They've no time for us little pests
They practise all on their billy
Coz they've no time to be playing silly
Singing all day
Singing all night
Just have a break to have a sip of Sprite
Then we shout, 'Hooray!'
But they don't want to just sing all day
They want to dance and sway all day
They don't just want to sing all day
Singing all day
Singing all night
Just have a break and have a sip of Sprite
Go backstage!
It's all gone a mess!
I think you'd better
Get redressed.
Singing all day
Singing all night
Just have a break to have a sip of Sprite!

Stacey Brown (10)
Rosehill Junior School, Rotherham

My Music

There is a flute in town
'Quick, quick look around'
It makes a sweet noise
But babies may think they are toys

I saw a clarinet but I knew it would frighten my pets
All way at home, all alone.

Terry Mitchell (10)
Rosehill Junior School, Rotherham

The Witches' School For Girls

'Miss, Miss, my broomstick's shaking
Please get me off.'
'I'm sorry dear, I'm sorry Miss
I've got a very bad cough.'

'Please, please
I'm gonna crash,'
'If it wasn't for you love
I wouldn't have any cash.'

'Come on love, come on love
Get off the floor,
Come on inside
Or else I'll lock the door.'

'Come on girls, it's dinnertime.'
'Ugh! This is gross,'
I've tried my best
I've made the most.

The headmistress
Miss What a *not!*
Ate somebody's sick
And soon forgot.

'Miss, Miss Maud's
hit me,'
'I need my glasses love
I cannot see.'

Tomorrow, tomorrow
I shall be free
I'll go down the slide
And shout 'Weeeeeeeeeee!'

Lauren Draycott (10)
Rosehill Junior School, Rotherham

Things I Do At School

Rip my work.
Put water on my t-shirt
Sing a song
All day long
Hit my leg
Don't nick a peg
Break my chair
Don't even care
Do my hair
Work in a pair
I lost my shoes
I need to go to the loo
I ran into the wall
Then I had a fall
Argh!
'Miss, I don't feel well,
I fell,
Ring my mum,
Can she come?
Please! Please!
It's not fair!
Don't you care?'

Chloe Darby (10)
Rosehill Junior School, Rotherham

Butterfly, Butterfly

Butterfly, Butterfly,
don't fly away.
Live in my garden,
I want you to stay.

I've tiny green bugs
all over my trees.
So come back, eat them
please!

Demi Wilkinson (8)
Rosehill Junior School, Rotherham

My Pet Goat

I have a pet goat and its
Name is Spot
And he sleeps in a shed
He wakes up with a moan.
My pet goat likes grass
Then he always stares
At glass
My pet goat looks like a bull
When it's mad, it acts like
It's full
When my goat is sad, it always
Moans with a groan.
My pet goat is like
A brother to me
When my pet goat
Is around my mum
Doesn't mind
And expects me to do
The grind.
My pet goat is with me
All the time.

Olivia Davies (8)
Rosehill Junior School, Rotherham

My Family

My family is full of surprise
My family is fun
A special day on holiday is in the sun
Always going running in the park
Families, families are smart
Families, families are so good
Some are good at sums
Some are good at being mums
You could have them around all day
They are always ready to play.

Danielle Easson (8)
Rosehill Junior School, Rotherham

Dancing

Dancing, dancing having fun
Put your hair up in a bun.

Twisting, turning all day long
Singing and dancing to a song.

Dancing, dancing having fun
Take out your very high bun.

Stop twisting and turning all day long
Stop singing and dancing to your song.

Stop dancing
Stop dancing
Stop having fun
Stop putting your hair up in a bun
Stop twisting
Stop turning all day long
Stop singing
Stop dancing to your song.

Aimee Jenkinson
Rosehill Junior School, Rotherham

Guitar

Play the guitar
Play the guitar
When you play the guitar
It makes a lovely sound
Make the sound loud
Make the sound quiet.

There are strings to pluck
Frets to press and keys to turn
Notes a, b, c, it sounds beautiful
To me!

Shelby Leigh Postans (9)
Rosehill Junior School, Rotherham

Under The Sea

I dive in the sea
With my goggles on tight
I don't go far down
So it's still very bright.

I open my eyes
It's so wonderful
I open my eyes
It's so colourful.

I look around
Pebbles shining
I look around
It's so exciting.

I swim to the left
A wonderful scene
I swim to the left
The sea deep bluey-green.

I look at a crab
Pincers sharp as a knife
I look at some more
It's so full of life.

Emily Huddleston (9)
Rosehill Junior School, Rotherham

Numeracy

Numeracy, numeracy is the best
Of the rest.
I think it's cool, especially at school.
Sums to do, I'm better than you
My friends ask me for answers in a test
Because I am the best.

Luke Riley (10)
Rosehill Junior School, Rotherham

Dancing

Twirling, twirling up and down
Dance to the music, round and round
Jump up and down to the sound
Do the splits, do the splits

5,6,7,8
Put your arms in the air
Ooh, Ooh
Put your arms in the air
Ooh, ooh.

Twirly, twirly
Round and round, up and down
Down and up
Glide, glide, glide.

Fly like a bird
Pounce like a tiger
Slither like a snake
Jump up and down like a kangaroo.

Can you twirl?
Can you spin?
Can you jump?
Can you do the splits?

Do the dance
Do the dance
Come on with me come on and
Dance!

Bethany Casterton (9)
Rosehill Junior School, Rotherham

About School

Wake up, wake up
School time, school time
Brush your teeth, brush your teeth
Iron your clothes, iron your clothes
Put them on, put them on
Butter your bread, butter your bread
Get the ham, get the ham
Put it in your lunchbox, put it in your lunchbox
Half-past eight, half-past eight
Time to go, time to go
Shoot through the door, shoot through the door
Run to school, run to school
Line up, line up
Teachers, teachers open the door, open the door
In we go, in we go
Take your shoes off, take your shoes off
Go to class, go to class
Find a seat, find a seat
'Morning Miss', 'Morning Miss'
After that, after that
Read a book, read a book
Bell rings, bell rings
Assembly, assembly
Sing a song, sing a song
Go out to play, go out to play
All day, all day
Half-past three, half-past three
Time to go, time to go
School's over, school's over
Go back home, go back home.

Sam Spink (10)
Rosehill Junior School, Rotherham

I Met A Frog And A Dog

I went to the park
I drew a big mark

Next I went home
Just in my dome

In the morning I awake
To find out I was wet as a slate

I got out of bed and fell on the floor
I went forward and opened the door.

I went to the park again
The mark looked quite mean
Not like a decorated game
Just then I saw a dog
And a frog
Just right on the mark.

Alisia Angel (8)
Rosehill Junior School, Rotherham

Pens, Pens, Pens

Pens for writing
Pens for drawing
Pens for highlighting
It's never boring.

There are lots of pens that you can chose from
Fat and thin
Long and short
Ink and ballpoint
　　　　　But!
Whatever pens are in your top ten
The best of them all, is a handwriting pen.

Alexandra Hetherington (10)
Rosehill Junior School, Rotherham

The Rosehill Park Poem

Children playing on the swings
Happily looking at nature's things.
Toddlers zooming down the slide
Thinking they are a paraglide
The noise of the swing in my ear
I see a teenager drinking beer.

As the golden sand burns in the sun
I see a young child scoff a bun.

As the grass cutter passes by I see
A young child start to cry.
I see a bird fly by and a
Girl thought she'd died.

Children working in the school while
Teenagers trash the swimming pool
Then suddenly I heard a noise I just thought it was the boys
I went to the toilet for a wee
And found that it was a bee.
I was scared of the bees
So I scared them away with a great big sneeze.

Jack Sheeran (11)
Rosehill Junior School, Rotherham

How To Make A Garden Grow

How to make a garden grow,
Plant a seed in gentle compost
Care for it like a baby that wakes up every morning
Give it a watering can full of water
Give it a breakfast of soil and water
Let the sun shine upon the seeds
Tell the rain to trickle down the leaves
And petals of the flower
And it will sound as the heavens are crying
And letting it rain.

Hannah Reeder (10)
Rosehill Junior School, Rotherham

Hobbies

Cricket is boring
It makes you fall asleep snoring,
Tennis is OK
On a beautiful day
Fishing is boring
Except when the fish are falling
Rugby is good
Especially when you see blood
Snooker is amazing
When the sun is blazing
Badminton is boring
When the rain is pouring
Football is the best
Much better than the rest!

Matthew Johnson (10)
Rosehill Junior School, Rotherham

School

Pencils are for drawing
Sometimes it's boring

Pens are for writing
Not for highlighting

Rulers are for underlining
Teachers are whining

Rubbers are for rubbing out
If I lose one I get a clout

When we get home we get a treat
But when we are at school
We don't get a sweet.

Isabella Cullen (10)
Rosehill Junior School, Rotherham

People And Excuses At School

'Miss, I spilt my water
Miss, my pen leaked
Miss, I need to be smarter
Miss, he has peeked.'

'Mrs I am trying
Mrs, my friend is hurt
Mrs, my friend is crying
Mrs, I ripped my skirt.'

'Mr can you sing?
Mr my bottle broke
Mr, are you the king?
Mr do you smoke?'

'Dinner lady, I want spaghetti
Dinner lady I want ash
Dinner lady are you called Ettie?
Dinner lady I want mash.'

'Helper I can't spell
Helper I can't write
Helper are you called Mel?
Helper I don't bite.'

Hayley Dudill (10)
Rosehill Junior School, Rotherham

Best Friends

Best friends forever you and me
We fell out and soon you'll see
We got back together after a while
And soon I saw that
Friends make you smile.

Lauren Longson (9)
Rosehill Junior School, Rotherham

My Three Best Friends

My three best friends
My best friends are very special to me
There always there when I need them
They help me when I'm troubled
And make me feel magical!

My best friends are really kind!
They're funny everyday
They make me feel cheerful all the time
And they are important

My best friends are most exciting
They're so wonderful to me
They always have a smile
And they're the best in the world!

My best friends are
Emily H, Jackie and Paige.

Amy Barrie (9)
Rosehill Junior School, Rotherham

Football

Football is good to play
I know I am very good
Score a goal and it is 1-1
I'm their best player on the ball.

Football crazy
Soccer mad, he used to
Play football when he
Was a little lad.

Joshua Willows (9)
Rosehill Junior School, Rotherham

Things I Have Been Doing Lately

Things I have been doing lately . . .
I've been scoffing great big cakes
Cutting my hair with the kitchen scissors
Doing stunts on my mini scooter
Trying to break my arm on the bed
Collecting fairies in a big old boot
Playing, spinning fizzy bottles.
Which makes me dizzy and bang my head
Pick the paint off my bedroom wall
Practising graffiti on the garage door
Doing my signature with the shampoo
Rolling the rabbit in chocolate spread
Biting my knees while watching TV
Blowing bubbles with chewing gum
Holding my breath in a smelly bath
Going to the toilet while watching TV!
Eating spaghetti from the microwave
Saving the best till last.

Aimee Morton (10)
Rosehill Junior School, Rotherham

Animal Craze

Cats are elegant felines with distinguished markings
Worshipped by the Egyptians
Owls with moonlight eyes glowing endlessly
Make good predictions
Armadillos a sandy colour
Scaly like they're dressed in armour.
Koalas from Down Under, harnessed on a tree
And munching on eucalyptus leaves
Always receives its dinner.

Hedgehogs are prickly like a thorn
Stay awake dusk till dawn.

Jana Thompson (10)
Rosehill Junior School, Rotherham

Sports

Bang, bang, bang
Goes a basketball.

Shoot, shoot, shoot
Shooting into the net.

Splash, splash, splash
Swimming in a race.

Blow, blow, blow
Whistle blows.

Argh, argh, argh
Ice-cold water.

Bang, shoot, splash
Blow, argh!
Yeah we won!

Lucie Tyler (10)
Rosehill Junior School, Rotherham

Sounds

The quietest sound in the world
Must be the tap, tap, tap
Of a walking ant.

The most scariest sound in the world
Must be a witch
Chuckling in the darkness.

The loudest sound in the world
Must be an avalanche falling.

The merriest sound in the world
Must be a baby laughing with me.

Sam Billups (10)
Rosehill Junior School, Rotherham

The Park

Sometimes . . . quiet
Sometimes . . . noisy
Sometimes . . . really loud.

Sometimes . . . tidy
Sometimes . . . messy
Sometimes . . . really messy
And quite tidy.

Sometimes . . . branches
Hanging off sometimes . . .
Leaves falling off.

People don't care
A bit about the
Park, they wouldn't
Be without.

Sophie Whittam (11)
Rosehill Junior School, Rotherham

Sunshine

Sunshine every day
Wake up now
Before it's your lucky day

Wind
Wind comes now
In your face
Give it up before it's
Your birthday.

Rain comes everyday
Cheer up soon enough!

Lauren Bateman (8)
Rosehill Junior School, Rotherham

Dinosaur Dream

Dinosaur's dream to be a car
But they are like a door
No one says they break the law
But they never catch a claw

Dinosaur, dinosaur is so fat
But I can never pat
But you never sat
And you don't eat a cat.

Joe Moore (7)
Rosehill Junior School, Rotherham

Ladybird, Ladybird

Ladybird, ladybird
Fly away home
Your house is on fire
And your children
Are gone
All except one and
That is Ann
She has crept
Under the frying pan.

Elizabeth M Stringer (8)
Rosehill Junior School, Rotherham

Snake

Snakes, snakes having fun
Biting moving all day long

Slithering, moving just for fun
Big snakes, small snakes
Wriggling on the ground

Slimy snakes, scaly snakes
Writhing all around.

Charly Manion (10)
Rosehill Junior School, Rotherham

My Kitten

My pet kitten is 3 months old
And I think that is as good as gold
It likes drinking and eating
And it dances to a beat
And I think it needs a treat
It is black and white
And she is always asleep
When she wakes up she likes a peep
And she likes to leap.

Harry Attwood (8)
Rosehill Junior School, Rotherham

Water Fights

On a lovely summer's day, all I ever do is play
Today I'm having a water fight I've got my bikini alright
I now fill up my swimming pool I hope it's really cool
I now fill up the water bombs and put them in a bucket
I now fill up buckets of water and put them in a row
And now that all my friends are here
I wet them head to toe!

Rosie Price (9)
Rosehill Junior School, Rotherham

Stars

Stars, stars, gleaming in the night
Stars, stars, like a flying kite
Stars, stars, shiny and gold
Stars, stars, are never ever cold
Stars, stars, gleam in the sky
Stars, stars, always die
Stars, stars, looking over you
Stars, stars, become new.

Bethany Watt (10)
Rosehill Junior School, Rotherham

My Fish

My fish is a goldfish
It has a scaly body and
Some bones and some stones
At the bottom of his tank

It likes to swim really fast
And it goes like a blast
It eats fish food
His name is called Fred
And he has a bed

He gets into trouble
By blowing big fat bubbles.

Tyler David Scothern (8)
Rosehill Junior School, Rotherham

My Pet Cat

My pet cat
Smells like a rat
His name is Harry
Harry's nickname is Barry
Harry eats fish
In a dish
My cat is fat
My cat eats rats
At the end of the day
My cat will play
And sleeps away.

Chloe Mae Davies (8)
Rosehill Junior School, Rotherham

Cat Doing Everything

Cat, cat playing footie but
Decides to eat Tom's bread butty
Cat, cat laying on the mat
Saw a rat and ate the bat and
Made himself a big fat cat
The rat tries not to go near
But he does and shuffles his ear
The cat muffles and that was
The end of that poor little rat
Tom says, 'What have you done?
You ate my bread butty
The rat and the bat and you are
Sat there big and fat.'

Luke Grainger (10)
Rosehill Junior School, Rotherham

My Dog and Rats

My pet dog can ride a scooter with
A hare and a bear
My two pet rats are very smart
They can ride on a sort of cart
One that I bought

My dog looks like a big stinky hog
And when he sees a bee he will start to be mean
My rats look like they are rocks and sometimes locks
When my rats see a fly they pretend to die.

Shellie O'Connor (8)
Rosehill Junior School, Rotherham

Rats

Rats, she got there first
Rats, how come she goes
Rats, she does everything
Rats, she is always in my room
Rats, how come she gets to do it
Rats, I am…not going this time
Rats, she has to go it is my turn
Rats, it was your turn last
Rats, she is always on
Rats, I want to watch a DVD
Rats, it's my turn to watch
Rats, it was your turn last time
Rats, I need to use that *now!*
Rats, she is always on the phone
Rats, she does things I want to
Rats, she always goes out
Rats, what about me? I need to go out
Rats, she always gets money
Rats, it's never fair Mum
Rats, she is always there
Rats, I want to crash the car
Rats, she gets me done for nothing
Rats, I want £70 for my birthday
Rats, she calls me mad
Rats, she gets a job paper I want that
Rats, she gets everything she wants
Rats, she never wants to do that
Rats, I want that, I want it!
Rats, she has got something of mine
Rats, make her do the washing up.

Alexandra Gregory (10)
Rosehill Junior School, Rotherham

The Dragons

Dragons, dragons scare you in the night
Dragons, dragons scare you with a fright
Eat the big delicious meat
And smell your big feet
Come out to play and
Have a lay
His name is Robert
Like a big slobert
He is big
Like a twig
When he read a book
He takes a big juicy look
Cause he is in a castle
He is not much hassle
Because he is in the castle in a tower
He moans hour by hour
Dragons, dragons in the night
Dragons scare you with a fright.

Ashley Spooner (9)
Rosehill Junior School, Rotherham

The Sound Of The Rain

The rain is fast
The rain is slow
The rain goes pitter-patter down the drain it goes
When it comes down slow
It sounds like a tap dancing show
It bounces off the roof tops
It bounces off the trees
It bounces on the playground
And then bounces on me.

Lauren Hudson (10)
Rosehill Junior School, Rotherham

Jungle Mania

I saw a monkey stuck up a tree
He screamed and growled and frightened me.

I saw a lion with big jaws
With very sharp nails on the end
Of his paws.

I saw a snake hissing in the tree
I looked up and he was staring at me.

Chloe Pashley (10)
Rosehill Junior School, Rotherham

Sport

I like to go swimming
And feel like I am winning
The water is so cold
And it will not scold
I was swimming under water to get the brick
Suddenly I heard a little click
I turned around and found a stick.

Emma Harrington (8)
Rosehill Junior School, Rotherham

Planes

In the airport there are lots of planes about
When we get on, my sister will scream and shout
It's fun and there's not much sun inside
But who cares? It's a lovely ride
Planes, planes everywhere
One is landing from the air
One taking off into the sky
The captain says, 'Get ready to fly.'

Jack Foss (8)
Rosehill Junior School, Rotherham

The Sun

The sun is big and sometimes small
And it reminds me of a big juicy bun
All day long I have some fun in the sun
The sun is round and about to bound
So move out of the way so you don't get blown today
The sun is reloading because it's going to be exploding
And the sun is a big ball of fire like a tyre
My mum is dry and I like to spy
Our flowers get powers from the sun
We have a water fight in the bright current bun.

Joshua Gillespie (8)
Rosehill Junior School, Rotherham

My Pet

My pet dog likes to sit on a rug
She eats and she eats until she falls asleep
My pet dog is not very old
Sometimes in the winter
She gets a bad cold
My pet dog likes a treat to eat
At teatime she gets hungry
This happens every day
'Woof, woof' she would say.

Nicole Tonks (8)
Rosehill Junior School, Rotherham

Space

S un, a burning dwarf star
P lanets, twinkling from afar
A stronaut goes into space
C omets falling with such grace
E arth is such a wonderful place.

Jack Oliver Dowell (10)
Rosehill Junior School, Rotherham

My Family

I have a family
And I have a brother
Who acts like a maniac
And my sister is a brainiac
My mum always laughs and
My dad always groans
I lay on the sofa my head surrounded
By pillows and I always moan

I have some friends and they never end
They are so kind and gentle
And always go with me
Wherever I go.

Olivia May Greenwood (8)
Rosehill Junior School, Rotherham

Skegness

I went to Skegness
We had lots of treats
I also won a game
That gave me loads of sweets
I went on the seaside
It was great fun
We had something delicious
Because it was a bun
When I went to Skegness
I thought I saw Loch Ness
I ate big candyfloss
It looked like big green moss.

Micah Drakes (8)
Rosehill Junior School, Rotherham

Achoo, Achoo, Achoo

Walking through the calm and soothing park
Birds start twittering cheerfully
Flying in the blue sky
They land on huge trees
The trees begin to sway
From side to side.
As my hay fever starts
To come up
The grass cutter begins
To come closer
My eyes start to water
The sneezing starts to begin.
Achoo, Achoo, Achoo!

Lauren Dickinson (10)
Rosehill Junior School, Rotherham

Football Poem

Football is good
Football is fair
And most of all my football is
Flying through the air.
I like playing football, it is fun
I mostly like it in the sun
And with a juicy bun
I play it in the park
With my friends
So my relationship never ends
I play in the park, am till pm
Until it is very dark.

Joshua Mason (8)
Rosehill Junior School, Rotherham

A Walk In The Park

The birds are singing
Trees are whistling
Leaves are crunching
Caterpillars munching.

The children are playing
Swings are swinging
The sand pit is drying
And babies are crying
Couples walk hand in hand
As children play up in the bandstand.

As I glare upon the trees
I feel an ever so slight summer's breeze
And the buzzy bees and whizzy wasps
Get knocked to the ground
By the big heavy raindrops
Lush green grass and ripe tall trees
Lets my hayfever make me sneeze.

Matthew Tonks (11)
Rosehill Junior School, Rotherham

My Pet Dragon

I have a pet dragon
His name is Spark
He lights up the place when it is dark
He sleeps in the shed in the backyard
His skin and his horns are so hard
I feed him in the morning and at night
But when I see him in broad daylight
He gives me such a fright
His horns are so sharp and his eyes are light green
When he sees people he is very mean
Me and my dragon are best friends
Until my life ends.

Faye Braisby (8)
Rosehill Junior School, Rotherham

Seasons

Spring
When it's spring children start to play about
When they do they always shout
When it's spring, winter is no more
When the rain starts to pour.

Summer
When it's summer kids are always out
When it's summer the sun comes out
When it's summer the rain has gone
When it's summer, spring has gone.

Autumn
When it's autumn playtime is nearly up
When it's autumn I think of our old pup
When it's autumn the leaves start to fall
When it's autumn time to throw snowballs.

Winter
When it's winter children don't play around
On the streets there is no sound
Winter is very, very cold
While your cheeks are red and bold.

Jordan Battersby (9)
Rosehill Junior School, Rotherham

My Holiday

I like going on holiday because it is fun
The colours are beautiful as the sun
I like to walk on the beach and eat a peach
I go to the fair with my auntie Clair
The weather is fine so I can climb
We have a big water fight
In broad daylight
I watch the fireworks at night
And they are bright.

Brianna Staton (8)
Rosehill Junior School, Rotherham

The Tiger

(Based on 'The Tiger' by William Blake)

Tiger, tiger
Burning bright
Sleeping through the day to night
Waiting for the sun to set
Have you had your breakfast yet?

Tiger, tiger
Burning bright
Sleeping through the day to night
Waiting now to catch your prey
Fall asleep in the middle of the day!

Tiger, tiger
Burning bright
Sleeping through the day to night
Make no movement start to play
Got to get that tiger away!

Tiger, tiger
Burning bright
Sleeping through the day to night
Waiting for the sun to set
Have you had your breakfast yet?

Tiger, tiger
Burning bright
Sleeping through the day to night
Waiting for the sun to fall
What for breakfast? Have them all!

Tiger, tiger
Burning bright
Sleeping through the day to night
They're all gone now you've had your food
Eat your dinner, don't be rude.

Katie Spencer (10)
Rosehill Junior School, Rotherham

The Park Walk

One day I wandered through the park
And I heard a dog start to bark
Through my eyes I started to see
What a beautiful world was all around me.
Then the trees started to dance
I could sit here for hours just to stare and glance
I saw an ant looking for food
It was gallant and bold, but then rather rude.
It crawled down my pants and started to bite me
And then came along a big fat bee.
The bee and the ant called for help
So then I decided to give out a yelp
The bees came from the sky and stung my butt
The ants from the earth and the grass freshly cut
I took off my shoe and whacked the bees
But the ants started to climb my knees
Like a tree I stood real still
I was like a cat ready for the kill
The next thing I did, was like a kid
I wailed as I ran, but then hit a van.
Luckily for me I knew the man, who drove the van
He shook the ants off my legs
But I still had a few stuck in my kegs
He took me home, back to my mum
But then my mum slapped my bum
It turns out it was half-past eight
I was extremely late
My mum sent me to be without any supper
All she gave me was thirst quenching cuppa.

Jake Beavers (11)
Rosehill Junior School, Rotherham

Four Short Poems

As the grass sways slowly
Side to side, getting hot in
The burning sun and swaying
In the breeze.

Children play in the park
Whilst running in the hot
Summer breeze and sliding down
The slide happily.

Birds fly over treetops
Looking for its prey, glancing
Down at the long, bushy grass.

Glass glitters in the sunlight
Waiting to stab a child, as
The glass glitters in the heat and
Waits for its victim.

Lewis Routledge (11)
Rosehill Junior School, Rotherham

The Park

As I slowly stride through the park
I hear tiny voices appearing everywhere
The grass starts to move, the wind blows a little
When the children start to play
There is laughter everywhere

When the wind starts to blow
Insects come and go
Birds tweeting in their trees flying
Past in summer breeze
Butterflies fluttering through the
Little bushy trees waiting for the
Hot summer breeze.

Matthew Ambler (10)
Rosehill Junior School, Rotherham

In The Park

As the
Colourful
Astonishing trees
Sway to and fro
The long, rough roots
Continue to grow
Different trees all
Around
The same thing about
Them is they are
Stuck to the ground.

Many children in
The park
Journeyed to see
Their dog bark
People swinging in the
Swings
As all the birds
Around them begin
To sing . . .

Matt Allen (11)
Rosehill Junior School, Rotherham

Sounds

Different sounds from every direction
Up, down, left and right, cars
Going for a drive.
Birds singing, cars driving, people walking
Children playing, people crushing their food
Children going through the tunnel
Playing happily. Adults watching
Their children, people eating their picnic
A little ant approached me and I rolled over
And that little ant is now dead.

Jordan Lowe (10)
Rosehill Junior School, Rotherham

Seasons

Autumn is the time
That the golden leaves
Fall off trees.

We have joy
We have fun
We have seasons.

Winter is the time
That cream white snow
Is on the go

We have joy
We have fun
We have seasons.

Spring is the time
That all the flowers
Rise again

We have joy
We have fun
We have seasons.

Summer is the time
That golden rays
Make days so warm.

Kieron Phillips (9)
Rosehill Junior School, Rotherham

The Marvellous Park

As I look at the marvellous view,
That lies upon me
I see the beautiful conker trees
And a copper beech tree, swaying in the breeze.

The beautiful coloured birds
That are flying in the air
Singing sweetly to a song
So sweetly it's making me happier.

The gorgeous white daisies
Which are planted in the ground
There dancing so beautifully
As the wind sways around.

The cool calming breeze
Is blowing in my face
It's making me comfy
On a cool summer's day.

Mothers bringing their babies to the park
Playing happily as they come along
Children laughing full of joy
Fathers playing footie with the boys.

Jessica Underwood (11)
Rosehill Junior School, Rotherham

Spring Things

Birds twitter in the tall trees
Towering overhead
Singing their songs so sweetly
As the fly
Full of hope as they swoop down
To grab food.
Trees sway as the calm breeze carries their
Overlapping branches this way and that
Leaves fall gracefully as light as a feather
On the luscious green grass
Sounds of small babies crying
Fill the air
Rusty red swings that squeak
As they sway to and fro
Blossom falling down from a tree
Like confetti on a newly wed bride,
There stands a weeping willow
With very droopy branches
Like a young child shedding masses
Of long lasting tears
The sycamore tree is like a lolly
Thin bare trunk then a burst of leaves
The two huge beech trees tower over the whole park
Like huge giants
Traffic goes by not knowing what
Beautiful world is around them.

Charlotte Stringer (11)
Rosehill Junior School, Rotherham

The Park

Birds making nests in the long tall trees
Swaying to and fro in the summer breeze

Children on the swings going up and down
As men pick up litter off the ground

Children in the playground happily play
As people stroll on the hot summer day

Big heavy machinery cutting the grass
As people drop the dirty old trash

Traffic hidden out of view
They stop at traffic lights to form a queue

Noisy sirens from the speeding ambulance
As people stop and take a worried glance

The newly cut grass blows in the breeze
As my hay fever starts and then I sneeze

Mums with prams on their daily walk
As they take a nice stroll through the park

Children laughing as they go down the slide
While couples take on a romantic stride

Graffiti on the brick wall by bad teenagers
As children play unaware of all ages

The big chunky horse chestnut tree
It's growing conkers I hope they don't fall on me

I slowly walk out of the park
I don't want to leave but it's getting quite dark.

Adam Ian Bates (11)
Rosehill Junior School, Rotherham

The Park

Swaying trees
Cold breeze
Green moss covering
The old school building
Butterflies flitter
Leaves glitter
As the sun rises.

A pit filled with sand
It crumbles in your hand
There's a spiky acorn tree
When the wind blows there
Beautiful blossom to see
The swings are rusty
The wind gets gusty
As the golden sun goes down
The atmosphere gets quiet.

Sophie Hughes (11)
Rosehill Junior School, Rotherham

Pets At Home

P is for parrot that makes a loud noise!
E is for elephant with it's very big trunk
T is for tiger with it's very smooth fur
S is for snake, slimy and long

A is for ant, so small
T is for turtle with it's hard shell

H is for hippo with it's huge horns
O is for octopus with it's 8 legs
M is for mole, black and white
E is for the end of my poem.

Amy Illingworth (8)
St Joseph's RC Primary School, Halifax

Football Crazy

The fans are all coming
To see the match
The referee blows his whistle
To start the match

Here comes a chance
The crowd are screaming
It's a goal!
Hooray, hooray!

It's near the end of the game
The referee blows his whistle
Full time and the crowd are screaming
Some are sad some are happy.

Niall Cuttle (8)
St Joseph's RC Primary School, Halifax

Jewels

Ruby is red
Emerald is green
They are rarely ever seen

Topaz is orange
Pearl is pink
Their dazzling shine
Makes you blink

Diamonds are shiny
Sapphire are blue
I wish I had one
To give to you.

Georgia Egan (11)
St Joseph's RC Primary School, Halifax

Wrestling

John Cena will give you a lot of pain
He'll hit you with his big silver chain
He's got some knucks
They say 'Word Life
Don't mess, he'll get knife'

Kurt Angle's career is over
He got chucked on to concrete
From 20 feet in the air
He's got a broken leg
Thanks to the Big Show

Steve Austin is from Austin, Texas
He's the toughest of them all
He beat NWO member
Scott Hall
At Wrestle Mania XVIII

Test has his 'pump handle slam'
His big boat as well
He's taken over Scott Steiner's career
Thanks to Stacey Keibler
A steal chair, between the eyes

Kane used to be a masked man
But now he's taken it off
He's trying to seduce Lita
He wants to woo her
But Lita is Matt Hardy's

The Undertaker must be the scariest of them all
His eyes up in his brain
Paul Bearer at ringside
With that urn in his hand
So jealous, his evil brother Kane.

Ben Cole (11)
St Joseph's RC Primary School, Halifax

Stuff And Nonsense

Giant snake
Birthday cake
Large fries
Chocolate shake.

Flavoured beans
Dirty jeans
Bumble bees
Apple trees.

Smelly socks
Alarm clocks
Magic wands
Ballet shoes.

Clocks that tick
Newborn chicks
Easter eggs
Long legs.

Clare Armstrong (9)
St Joseph's RC Primary School, Halifax

I Lost My Ted

I lost my ted
In my bed
Under the sheet
With my smelly feet
I lifted the sheet
To take a peek
And my feet
Made such a wreak.

Robert Dickinson (9)
St Joseph's RC Primary School, Halifax

My Week And Weekend

Monday I play outside on my bike
Riding wherever I want
Tuesday I sit inside watching the rain
Dribbling down the windowpane
Wednesday sitting in the boiling sun
Watching the clouds go by
Thursday and sitting on a horse so big
Trotting along the road
Friday resting peacefully in my bed
Until morning rises
Saturday planting in the garden
Watching the flowers grow
Sunday I rest inside watching my television
Until night-time comes.

Laura Burton (9)
St Joseph's RC Primary School, Halifax

Fairytale Future

Where houses are gingerbread
Where eggs sit on walls
Where sheep are lost
Where the egg falls.

Where dolls come alive
Where swans turn to princesses
Where spirits fly
Where horses go by
Where the grass is sherbet
Where rags turn to riches
Where little girls work all day long
What happy ending
Will finish this song?

Charlotte Coyne (9)
St Joseph's RC Primary School, Halifax

In The Kitchen

K is for kagoule when it rains
I is for inside cooking tea
T is for tea time
C is for carrots and veg (yuk)
H is for heat wave
E is for eating desserts
N is for nearly finished.

Laura Whittaker (8)
St Joseph's RC Primary School, Halifax

Winter

Winter fires
Snow covers the land
A blistering breeze
Water frozen into ice
Frozen windows
Frozen hands.

John Paul Morrow (9)
St Joseph's RC Primary School, Halifax

Winter Poem

F rosty icicle
R olling snowmen
O utside people playing
S hutting doors quickly
T urning lakes into ice.

Reece Fisher Lowry (9)
St Joseph's RC Primary School, Halifax

Sunset

It is the end of the day
When we all sit down and pray
The blue sky turns to purple
The purple turns to black
Studded with silver earrings
The moon has come to say hello
To keep the city bright
Even though it's bright inside
And outside we have lights
Now it's time to wake
When the dawn and morning break.

Hayley Keane (9)
St Joseph's RC Primary School, Halifax

The Winter Poem

W is for winter is coming
 I is for ice on the roads and cars
N is for November when the snow is coming
T is for temperature when it is low
E is for everywhere covered with snow
R is for robins are near.

Matthew Bartey (9)
St Joseph's RC Primary School, Halifax

Snow And Summer (Haiku)

Creeping in the snow
Peeping here, there, everywhere
Summer is here now.

Harriet Slater (9)
St Joseph's RC Primary School, Halifax

A Winter Poem

Winter is cold
The snow is falling
Windows are frozen
Children are playing in the snow
They make snowmen
Cars are slipping
People sit around the fire.

Joe McGinley (9)
St Joseph's RC Primary School, Halifax

Promise Of Friendship

(Based on poem of same name by Pie Corbett)

I want to be friends with you
Till I see a blue monkey
Till tortoises can fly
And a cactus crawls into the city.

If we are friends
I will let you borrow my teddy bear
I will let you use the remote control
To my television.

I will give you
The juiciest berries
The warmth of the sun
And the sweetest apple in New York.

I will like you more than
My dream holiday in France
The rustling whisper of
Autumn leaves
And the delicious
Taste of spaghetti bolognese.

Sophie Coolledge (11)
Womersley CE Primary School, Doncaster

Promise Of Friendship

(Based on poem of same name by Pie Corbett)

I want to be friends with you
Till the alphabet begins with X
My eyes flash red and gold
And sugar tastes sour.

If we are friends
I will lend you my PlayStation 2
And let you borrow my big radio.

I will give you
my talking white robot from Spain
That moves and picks up toys.

I will like you more than
The splash of a mermaid's tail
The whoosh of going down a roller coaster
And a shiny apple.

Joshua Kneafsey (10)
Womersley CE Primary School, Doncaster